RIVERBANK AT BATOCHE, 1885

NOVEMBER 16, 1885

NO FEATHER, NO INK
AFTER RIEL

Thistledown Press

© Thistledown Press, 1985

Canadian Cataloguing in Publication Data

Main entry under title:
    No feather, no ink

Poems.
ISBN 0-920633-02-1 (bound).
ISBN 0-920633-03-X (paperback).

1. Canadian poetry (English)* 2. Riel, Louis, 1884-1885 — Poetry.
3. Riel Rebellion, 1885 — Poetry. I. Amabile, George, 1936-
II. Dales, Kim, 1955-
PS8287.R53N6 1985   C811'.008'0351   C85-091328-4
PR9195.85.R53N6 1985

Book design by A.M. Forrie
Paintings by Henry Letendre
Typesetting by Pièce de Résistance, Edmonton
Set in 11 point Century Oldstyle

Printed and bound in Canada by
Hignell Printing Limited, Winnipeg

Thistledown Press
668 East Place
Saskatoon, Saskatchewan
S7J 2Z5

LOUIS RIEL, 1884

CONTENTS

ACKNOWLEDGEMENTS

Every effort has been made to contact copyright owners of material used herein. In the case of errors or omissions, the publishers would be grateful for any information enabling suitable acknowledgements to be made in the future.

MILTON ACORN. 'Dig Up My Heart' from *Dig Up My Heart* (McClelland & Stewart, 1983) by Milton Acorn. Reprinted by permission. PATRICK ANDERSON. 'The Country Still Unpossessed' from 'Poem on Canada' in *The White Centre* by Patrick Anderson. Used by permission of Orlando L.F. Gearing. MARGARET ATWOOD. From *Survival: A Thematic Guide to Canadian Literature* by Margaret Atwood (Toronto: House of Anansi Press, 1972). Reprinted by permission. E.D. BLODGETT. 'for ducks' from *Beast Gate* (NeWest Press, 1980) by E.D. Blodgett; 'Métis' from *Arché/Elegies* (Longspoon Press, 1983) by E.D. Blodgett; and 'omphalos' all reprinted by permission of the author. GEORGE BOWERING. 'Uncle Louis' from *West Window* by George Bowering. Reprinted by permission of George Bowering and Stoddart Publishing Company Ltd., Toronto, Canada. ELIZABETH BREWSTER. Reprinted by permission of Oberon Press: 'At Batoche' from *The Way Home* by Elizabeth Brewster. MICK BURRS. 'Under the White Hood' from *Moving in from Paradise* by Mick Burrs. Reprinted by permission of the author. BARBARA CASS-BEGGS. Translation of 'Chanson de Louis Riel' from *Seven Métis Songs* (BMI, 1967) by Barbara Cass-Beggs, and 'Chanson de Riel' translated by Father Rufin Turcotte and collected by Barbara Cass-Beggs. Reprinted by permission. JOHN ROBERT COLOMBO. 'The Last Words of Louis Riel' © John Robert Colombo 1967, reprinted from *Abracadabra* with permission; 'Louis Riel (After Miroslav Holub)' © John Robert Colombo 1974, reprinted from *The Sad Truths* with permission. LORNA CROZIER. 'Drifting Towards Batoche' used by permission of the author. KIM DALES. 'Duck Lake Massacre', 'Fort Saskatchewan, 1884' and 'How My Great Uncle Missed Most of the Riel Rebellion' used by permission of the author. FRANK DAVEY. 'Riel' from *The Louis Riel Organ and Piano Company* (Turnstone Press, 1985) by Frank Davey. Reprinted by permission of the author. DAVID DAY. 'Captain Kilroy Was Here' from *The Scarlet Coat Serial* (Press Porcepic, 1981) by David Day. Reprinted by permission of the author. R.G. EVERSON. 'The Métis' from *Selected Poems* (Delta, 1970) and 'Riding North Towards Duck Lake, Sask.' used by permission of the author. DON FREED. 'Duck Lake' © Don Freed 1983. Used by permission of the author. JOHN GLASSCO. Translation of 'From *A Sir John A. MacDonald*' © John Glassco 1970. Reprinted by permission of W.E. Toye. DAVID GODFREY. 'Thirty One: Influence' and 'Forty Nine: Revolution' from *I Ching Kanada* (Press Porcepic, 1976) by David Godfrey, reprinted by permission. DON GUTTERIDGE. 'Riel' from *New Poems of the seventies* (Oberon, 1970). Used by permission of the author. TERRENCE HEATH. 'Lament of Madeleine Dumont, July, 1885' used by permission of the author. BRUCE HUNTER. 'He Encounters Hostility in the West' from *Benchmark* (Thistledown Press, 1982) by Bruce Hunter. Reprinted by permission of the author and Thistledown Press. CONNIE KALDOR. 'Maria's Place/Batoche' from the LP *Moonlight Grocery* by Connie Kaldor. Used by permission of the author. E.A. LACEY. 'Saudade' from *Patter of Snow* (Catalyst, 1974) by E.A. Lacey. Used by permission. PATRICK LANE. 'For Riel in that Gawdam Prison' from *Poems New and Selected* (Oxford University Press, 1978) by Patrick Lane. Reprinted by permission of the author. DOROTHY LIVESAY. 'Prophet of the New World: A Poem for Voices' from *Collected Poems* (Ryerson Press, 1972) by Dorothy Livesay. Reprinted by permission of the author. JAMES A. MacNEILL. 'A Métis Child Dies' from *Prairiefire* (Western Extension College 1976). Reprinted by permission of the author. DAVID McFADDEN. 'The Opening of the West' from *My Body Was Eaten by Dogs* (McClelland & Stewart, 1981) by David McFadden. Reprinted by permission of the author. KEN MITCHELL. 'The Nile' used by permission of the author. ERIN MOURÉ 'Riel: In the Season of His Birth' from *Empire, York Street* by Erin Mouré (Toronto: House of Anansi Press, 1979). Reprinted by permission. JOHN NEWLOVE. 'Ride Off Any Horizon' and 'Crazy Riel' from *Black Night Window* (McClelland & Stewart, 1968) by John Newlove. Reprinted by permission of the author. BP NICHOL. 'The Long Weekend of Louis Riel' from *Craft Dinner* (Aya Press, 1978) by bpNichol. Reprinted by permission of the author. DON POLSON. 'Canadian Heyday' from *Lone Travellers* (Fiddlehead, 1979) by Don Polson. Reprinted by permission of the author. CRAIG POWELL. 'Sunday Morning in St. Boniface' from *Rehearsal for Dancers* (Turnstone Press, 1978) by Craig Powell. Reprinted by permission of the author and Turnstone Press. E.J. PRATT. 'Hollow Echoes from the Treasury Vault', a section of 'The Last Spike' by E.J. Pratt, reprinted by permission of University of Toronto Press. AL PURDY. Reprinted by permission of McClelland & Stewart: 'The Battlefield at Batoche' from *Sex and Death* by Al Purdy; 'Canadian Spring' from *Sundance at Dusk* by Al Purdy. KEVIN ROBERTS. 'Riel' used by permission of the author. GLEN SORESTAD. 'The Ravens' and 'Archaeologists at Batoche' from *Ancestral Dances* (Thistledown Press, 1979) by Glen Sorestad. Reprinted by permission of the author and Thistledown Press; 'Fish Creek' from *Hold the Rain in Your Hands* (Coteau Books, 1985) by Glen Sorestad reprinted by permission of the author. RAYMOND SOUSTER. Reprinted by permission of Oberon Press: 'Riel, 16 Novembre, 1885' from *Collected Poems vol. 2* (1981) by Raymond Souster; 'The Heroes' and 'Found Poem: Louis Riel Addresses the Jury' from *Extra Innings* (1977) by Raymond Souster. GEORGE F.G. STANLEY. Translation of 'Dumont's Account of the North West Rebellion' from *Canadian Historical Review* vol. 30, September 1949. Reprinted by permission of the author and University of Toronto Press. ANDREW SUKNASKI. 'Gabriel Dumont and an Indian Scout Changing Coats' and 'Blood Red the Sun' from *The Ghosts Call You Poor* (Macmillan, 1978) by Andrew Suknaski reprinted by permission of the author; 'Letter to Big Bear' from *The Land They Gave Away* (NeWest Press, 1982) by Andrew Suknaski reprinted by permission of the author and NeWest Press. GAEL TURNBULL. 'Riel' from *A Gathering of Poems* (Anvil Press, 1983) by Gael Turnbull reprinted by permission of Anvil Press. GEOFFREY URSELL AND BARBARA SAPERGIA. 'South Saskatchewan' used by permission of the authors. MIRIAM WADDINGTON. 'The Visitants' © Miriam Waddington 1981 reprinted from *The Visitants* (Oxford University Press) with permission. CHRISTOPHER WISEMAN. 'At Fort Qu'Appelle' from *An Ocean of Whispers* (Sono Nis Press, 1983) by Christopher Wiseman reprinted by permission of the author. GEORGE WOODCOCK. 'On Completing a Life of Dumont' from *Collected Poems* (Sono Nis Press, 1983) by George Woodcock. Reprinted by permission of Sono Nis Press. WINSTON WUTTUNEE. 'Ride, Gabriel, Ride' from *Songs of the Northwest* (Sunshine Records). Transcribed by Annette Floyd and used by permission of the author.

Illustration of the battle at Duck Lake on page 25 (photographed by Donna Sorestad) and ad copy for T. Thompson & Sons on page 26 (photographed by Richard Gustin) are from *Illustrated War News* vol. 1, no. 1, 4 April 1885. The original document is housed in the Prairie History Room, Regina Public Library. The photos of Louis Riel on pages 7 and 51 are reproduced courtesy of the Saskatchewan Archives. The photo of Gabriel Dumont on page 16 is reproduced courtesy of the Public Archives of Canada (C-27663).

Thistledown Press would like to acknowledge the work of George Amabile and Kim Dales

The publisher assumes final editorial responsibility for the book.

This book has been published with the assistance of the North West Centennial Advisory Committee, the Saskatchewan Arts Board, and the Canada Council.

The difference between the Bible and Canada is that in the Bible God helps, miracles happen, David wins. But Riel's defeat is absolute, and unlike Brebeuf he doesn't even get to be a tourist attraction.

—from *Survival* by Margaret Atwood

GABRIEL DUMONT, CIRCA 1885

GABRIEL DUMONT
(TRANSLATED BY GEORGE F.G. STANLEY)
Dumont's Account of the North West Rebellion

On March 25th, 1885, being at St. Antoine de Padoue, which is half a mile from Batoche, when the mounted police appeared on the other side of the river, I asked Riel to give me 30 men so that we could go to Duck Lake and ransack our opponents' storehouses. When I got there, Mitchell[6] had fled. I got Magnus Burnstein,[7] his clerk, to give me the keys to his warehouse, and helped myself to the contents.

I then left with ten men to reconnoitre the road to Carlton, taking care to send scouts in advance.

After midnight, my scouts, Baptiste Ouellet and Baptiste Arcand, saw two men on horseback go by, Ross and Astley.[8] My brother Edouard, Philippe Gariépy,[9] Baptiste Deschamps, an Indian and I pursued them. Although my men were armed, I gave orders that they were not to harm anyone who did not resist.

We caught up to them at Duck lake, and I swooped down upon them. I took aim at them saying in Indian: "Don't try to escape, or I'll kill you". Ross said to me "I'm a surveyor". I knocked him down off his horse. Seeing his revolver, I grabbed it from him, telling him "You're no surveyor, you're a liar".

Astley escaped, and as my men wanted to kill him, I ordered them not to do anything to him. However, he fell off his horse and they seized him. We took them both disarmed to Duck Lake, and kept them prisoners. I told them that if they behaved, they would be well treated.[10]

We took possession of their horses.

This man Ross whom I had taken into custody in this manner was a sheriff. He must have been very frightened because, in his testimony, he said we numbered fifty[11] when there were only 5 of us. He also claimed in the same testimony that his companion had kept him from shooting, he certainly didn't have time to do so, because I jumped on him too fast.

We were going out to stable our horses when someone shouted: "Here come the police", but it was only three scouts whom my brother Edouard, Patrice Fleury, my brother-in-law James Short,[12] and I chased and who escaped. Patrice Fleury said he saw Mackay[13] among those scouts.

My companions had a lead over me in the chase after the fugitives, and I realized that they had fallen into an ambush of some forty mounted policemen who were taking aim at them. I galloped my charger towards my comrades shouting at them to get off their horses. I myself dismounted, because I heard a sergeant swear he was going to kill me. I immediately aimed at him yelling "It is I who will kill you". Then he emptied his rifle, putting it across his knees. I promptly pounced on him and knocked him over with the barrel of my rifle. When I lifted my gun up again a shot went off by accident. Then Thomas Mackay rushed at me saying "Be careful Gabriel". I answered him, "You'd better be careful yourself, or I'll blow your brains out". And I flung myself upon him. He turned his horse which had its back feet sunk in snow, and it reared up. I gave Mackay a push in the back with my rifle. He spurred his horse and it gave a leap forward and got away. Meanwhile, Mackay kept telling me, "Watch out Gabriel" and I kept repeating too, "You'd better be careful yourself, or I'll slaughter you" and I followed him with my gun.

My brother had jumped into one of the police vehicles to capture the two men in it. But they whipped their horses and made him tumble out. The cart passed over him.

There were about twenty double-yoked sleighs, and there were two men in each. Mackay commanded the retreat. I shouted at him, "What did you come here for?" He replied that he had come to talk to us. "But don't run away like this," I answered him "we were told that you would come with men, Where are they? You're only one blockhead".[14]

When I saw they were going to run away, I stopped my men from running after them. They weren't numerous enough to check them, there were only three of them.

We went back to Duck Lake, and we had scarcely let our horses out to eat, when we heard someone shout again, "Here come the police". We immediately jumped on horseback, and without delay I had my men occupy a hillock when commanded the plain, and from where the enemy would have been able to level their guns on us.

We were only a few men on horseback and a few men on foot, waiting for the police who had been reinforced by eighty men commanded by Crozier, who had rejoined Mackay's forty runaways. They had a cannon with them.[15]

I sent in pursuit of their scouts several men to whom I gave orders not to shoot, because Riel had asked us not to be the first to fire.

I gave orders to my horsemen, who numbered 25, to go down into a hollow, where we were under shelter from the cannon.

Crozier, accompanied by an English half-breed, approached one of our Indians who was unarmed and, it seems, gave him his hand. The Indian then tried to grab the gun out of the hands of the English Métis who was, I believe, John Dougall Mackay. This English Métis fired, and I think it was this rifle shot which killed my brother Isidore and made him fall from his horse, stone dead.[16]

What makes me think that it was this shot which killed my brother is that this Métis had an interest in killing him, seeing that my brother was the only one armed.

As soon as the shot was fired, the police and the volunteers commanded by Crozier, fired a round, and the Indian who was with my brother, was killed.

All this happened without any parley taking place between the two sides.

Charles Nolin, who at first had been full of boasting, had come with us to the fight, against his will. At the first shot, he fled, taking his sister-in-law's cart, going off in the direction of Prince Albert where he gave himself up.[17]

As soon as the shooting started, we fired as much as we could. I myself fired a dozen shots with my Winchester carbine, and I was reloading it to begin again, when the English alarmed by the number of their dead,[18] began to withdraw. It was time they did, for their cannon which until then had kept my infantry men from descending the slope, was silenced because the gunner, in loading

19

it, put in the shot before the powder. My infantrymen then began to surround them.

This first encounter had lasted half an hour.

In their flight they had to go through a clearing, so I lay in wait for them saying to my men, "Courage, I'm going to make the red coats jump in their carts with some rifle shots". And then I laughed, not because I took any pleasure in killing, but to give courage to my men.

Since I was eager to knock off some of the red coats, I never thought to keep under cover, and a shot came and gashed the top of my head, where a deep scar can still be seen; I fell down on the ground, and my horse, which was also wounded, went right over me as it tried to get away. We were then 60 yards from the enemy. I wanted to get up, but the blow had been so violent, I couldn't. When Joseph Delorme saw me fall again, he cried out that I was killed. I said to him, "Courage, as long as you haven't lost your head you're not dead". I then told Bte Vandal to take my cartridges and my rifle which was famous and which had a range of 800 yards.

All during the battle, this Delorme was at my side fighting like a lion. But before the fight, he had said to me: "I have never been under fire, if I am afraid, don't spare me but keep me keyed up".

While we were fighting, Riel was on horseback, exposed to the gunfire, and with no weapon but the crucifix which he held in his hand.

Seeing me fall, my brother Edouard rushed forward to drag me down into the ravine, but I told him to go first to our men who seemed to be discouraged by my fall. He rallied them; they began to shout with joy and started shooting again. It was then my cousin Auguste Laframboise whom I had, only a few minutes before, been urging not to expose himself so much, fell close to my side. A bullet had struck his arm and passed through his body. I crawled and dragged myself over to him, saying to myself: "I am always going to say a little prayer for him", but wishing to make the sign of the cross with my left hand, since my right side was paralysed,

I fell over on my side and, laughing I said, "Cousin, I shall have to owe it to you".

I should have liked to say for him the prayer which I made up when we had been blessed by the priest at Belton, in Montana,[19] "Lord, strengthen my courage, my faith and my honour that I may profit all my life from the blessing I have received in Thy holy name".

This is an invocation which I have always said after my prayers, morning and night. This blessing we had received on leaving Montana had impressed Riel so much that he often asked me if I remembered it.[20]

When Riel saw Laframboise fall, he said to me, "Uncle, I am going to have our men on foot advance." I told him that would be like sending them into the lion's den, and that he would do better to maintain the morale of those still on the battle field.

The enemy was then beginning to retire, and my brother, who had taken command after my fall, shouted to our men to follow and destroy them. Riel then asked, in the name of God, not to kill any more, saying that there had already been too much bloodshed.

However, there was a captain whom the police called Morton,[21] a good shot, who was behind a tree and had killed two of our men; he was hit in the back while trying to get away. As he was screaming and suffering horribly, Guillaume Mackay thought he did him a service by shooting him in the head.

The retreating men left behind nine dead and one man wounded in the leg. Since this last man wanted to continue shooting, Philippe Gariépy threw himself on him, wrenched his gun and bayonet from him and tried to hit him with his weapon. One of our men restrained Gariépy, and urged him to have pity on the miserable creature who was taken to Duck Lake.

In the haste of their flight, Clarke[22] forgot to take along his wild cat fur cap.

The vanquished left behind 4 or 5 carts and 8 uninjured horses, as well as several dead ones. In their carts we found some stove tops behind which they had hidden while firing.

They did, however, remove the bodies of the dead mounted policemen, who could easily be recognized by their red uniforms, but they left on the ground the bodies of nine volunteers. I think they lost 16 men including captain Moore, who had a leg broken and amputated.[23]

After the enemy had fled, my companions tied me on my horse, and we went to Duck Lake, where my wound, which was a deep one, was dressed. They also brought in the carts.

We lost five men in this encounter: J.-Bte Montour, Joseph Montour, Auguste Laframboise, Isidore Dumont, and an Indian, Joseph Trottier (named after his godfather).

The next day, March 26, 1885, Riel assembled his forces in two ranks and said to them, "Give three cheers, Hurrah for Gabriel Dumont! Thank God who gave you so valiant a leader".

We spent the whole day in prayer for our dead whose bodies we laid out in a house. They were buried the next day at St. Laurent.

---

[6]Hillyard Mitchell, a trader at Duck Lake.

[7]Magnus Burston was subsequently tried for complicity in the rebellion but was discharged.

[8]Harold Ross, deputy sheriff at Prince Albert: John W. Astley, civil engineer and land surveyor resident at Prince Albert.

[9]Philippe Gariépy was later sentenced to seven years' imprisonment for complicity in the rebellion.

[10]Ross in his evidence at the trial of Louis Riel gave the following account of this incident: "Gabriel Dumont came to me and recognized me, and said how are you, you are a scout, and he told me to dismount, that I was his prisoner, and I refused to dismount, and they pulled me off the horse. They were all armed, every one of them. Gabriel Dumont then felt my revolver, he felt it under my coat, he got quite excited, and he went to take it away from me, and I drew the revolver out myself, and he held it, (witness showing how it was held holding his right hand to his stomach) and I was covered by an Indian on my right with a gun, and there were two more behind me. Guns were pointed at me, and Mr. Astley called on me not to shoot, better hand over the revolver" (The Queen vs Louis Riel, Ottawa, 1886, 34).

Astley's account was as follows: "I was about thirty or forty yards on ahead of Ross, and an Indian suddenly jumped alongside of me and pointed his rifle or shotgun at my breast.

I turned around to see if my partner was prisoner too. I saw that he was, and that there were some sixteen or twenty of them all armed, and, as he was captured first, I thought it was best to give up quietly'' (ibid., 27).

[11]Ross said ''We were taken prisoners by Gabriel Dumont and between sixty and one hundred men'' (ibid., 34).

[12]James Short was given seven years in the penitentiary for complicity in the rebellion.

[13]Thomas McKay, Scotch half-breed, resident of Prince Albert. Immediately prior to the rebellion McKay and Mitchell acted on behalf of Superintendent Crozier in negotiations with Riel (G.F.G. Stanley, *The Birth of Western Canada*, London, 1936, 324-5).

[14]McKay's account of this episode was as follows: ''I was told that Crozier wanted to send sergeant Stewart with teams, and an escort for the purpose of getting some provisions and flour from the store belonging to Mitchell, at Duck Lake, and that he wanted me to accompany the party, and we were to start at four o'clock the next morning, that would be the 26th. The next morning came and we got up and got ready, sergeant Stewart sent out an advance guard of four men on ahead towards Duck Lake, to see if the road was clear; we followed with the teams and sleighs. I was riding on about a quarter of a mile ahead of the teams looking out. When I got within three or four miles of Duck Lake, I noticed some people lying in the snow, there were marks, I took them to be Indians. I noticed them communicating the signal by walking backwards and forward; I suspected they were watching the trail. I got within about a mile and a half of Duck Lake; there is a ridge there a little to the north of the mail station; when I got there I saw some mounted policemen riding at full galop, and immediately after them there were some mounted men, following them; I wheeled around and rode back as hard as I could make my horse go. There was a hill about a quarter of a mile away, I wanted to get there before they came. When I got within sight of the men I threw up my hands and told them to prepare and get their rifles ready. I told them that they were following the Mounted Police. I told them to get their rifles and said not to fire, whatever they do, I can ride out and if they want to fire they can have the first chance at me and you can defend yourselves. They were coming round the bluff, they were pretty close to the men, I saw they would overtake them, I knew they were excited, so I rode out as hard as I could, they then hauled up, all but one man who came right on and who never hauled up at all, it was Patrick Flary (Patrice Fleury). I asked them what they were about. They said: What are you about? I said we were going to Duck Lake, to get Mitchell's provisions. They said there were a great many there. I asked whether they were at Duck Lake and they said yes. They said we had better go back. I turned around and went towards the sleighs, as I was getting near the sleighs, a party of perhaps 30 or 40 of them very excited, came upon us; they were yelling and flourishing their rifles; they were very excited. Gabriel Dumont was of the party; he was very excited, jumped off his horse and loaded his rifle and cocked it, and came up to me and threatened to blow out my brains, he, and some others threatened to use their rifles; I told them to be quiet, that two could play at the game. Dumont talked very wildly, he wanted us to surrender. He said it was my fault that the people were not assisting them, and that I was to blame for all the trouble. I told him we could not surrender, that I thought we had the best right to this property. Some of them jumped off their horses and went into the sleighs. I rode up and told the teamster to hold on to his horses. They made one or two attempts to snatch the lines, finally he fired his rifle over our heads; they all stepped off the road and we went on the road to Carlton'' (The Queen vs Louis Riel, 21-2).

[15]Crozier's whole force numbered fifty-six North West Mounted Police and forty-three Prince Albert Volunteers, ninety-nine in all. Dumont gives them a strength of 120. They had a seven pounder gun with them.

[16]An account of this incident may be found in N.F. Black, *History of Saskatchewan and the Old North West* (Regina, 1913), 277. Black states that the first shot was fired by the interpreter Mackay, although Crozier claimed that the Métis fired first.

[17]Charles Nolin was a Red River Métis, who had taken part in the Red River Rising in 1869-70. In 1875 he entered the Norquay Cabinet as minister of agriculture. Subsequently he moved to the Saskatchewan valley. He disapproved strongly of Riel's decision to take up arms. Forced to go to Duck Lake with the Métis he took advantage of the first opportunity to escape and took refuge at Prince Albert. He was always opposed to extreme measures and represented the conservative element among the Métis. He died in 1907 and was interred at St. Boniface (Morice, *Dictionnaire historique*, 209-10).

[18]The militia and police had, by this time, suffered ten killed; two fatally wounded and eleven wounded. Five of their horses had been killed or disabled (Stanley, *Birth of Western Canada*, 328).

[19]Probably Fort Benton.

[20]This was the occasion of the invitation to Louis Riel, then teaching school in Montana, to return to Canada to champion the rights of the Métis of the Northwest. The invitation was borne to Riel by a delegation including Michel Dumas, Moïse Ouellet, James Isbister, and Gabriel Dumont.

[21]Captain John Morton, a farmer from Bruce County, Ontario, was a volunteer officer in the Prince Albert Volunteers (C.P. Mulvaney, *The History of the North West Rebellion of 1885*, Toronto, 1885, 32, 42-3).

[22]Lawrence Clarke, chief factor, Hudson's Bay Company, and member of the Council of the Northwest Territories for the district of Lorne.

[23]Captain H.S. Moore of the Prince Albert Volunteers.

Vol. 1, No. 13.   TORONTO, APRIL 4TH, 1885.   {10c. PER COPY.

ATEST NEWS.

April 1.—Nearly all the Sas-
ians are ready for pillage and
e Battleford people are still
. The Indians have suddenly
stern direction. They are not
y away long, and are probably
deserted farms near by. Col.
Regina to-day for the relief of
forty men and two field guns.
posed to raise 100 volunteers
erchmer, but his brother in
sed him that it was no use, as
not get through. It is feared
will have little chance to reach
he worst fears are entertained
s only twenty-five police and
re there, and nothing has been
em for several days. Com-
till cut off with Prince Albert,
t that settlement is safe. The
mpany's agent at Battleford
orning to secure stores across
r. Four rebels were loading
board, and under cover of the
nt captured the buckboard and
man. The agent found the
ttered, and removed what was
icks.

Dewdney is again at Fort Qu'-
ultation with Gen. Middleton.
ns at Oak Lake, west of Bran-
ted and loyal, and can be en-
Government side. The half-
ont ary, would assist Riel but
y. The mail route between
and Battleford cannot be
enr's ba d and the Fort Pitt
joined Riel. Montana half-
said to be taking p rt in the
ther Le Bret, of the Fort Qu'
n, says between 7,000 and
ed troops will be required to
ebellion. Many settlers at
other p aces have aba doned
ls, leaving everything to the
und-r and destroy everything
Settlers arr ving at Fort Qu'-
the north, report that their
as lit up at stretches with the
and houses. The Indian in-
ich more serious than the half-
account of their desperate
r motives being starvation,
r, and revenge on deceitful
enta. All the repeating rifles
n in St. Paul, Minneapolis,
r points have been sent for by
t.

and sacking of the town of
he Crees is confirmed. The
und Duck Lake are expected
ttack upon the barracks to be
he immediate direction of
Three bands of Crees are
on the south side of Battle-
xpected that Big Bear's band
Pitt Indians, numbering 800
join them, the meeting-place
of last summer's conflict with

April 1.—It is estimated that
between fifteen hundred and
men at his command. They
ell-armed, but the report that
pieces is untrue. It is un-
ie is receiving aid from the
me men have been seen with
t half-breeds, Indians or set-
rangers, entirely unacquainted
y. It is also rumored that he
.nsignment of dynamite, but
extremely improbable, as it is
erstand to what use he could

T. THOMPSON & SON

OUR GREAT SUMMER FAIR

—: AND THE :—

NORTH-WEST WAR

ARE THE TALK OF THE WHOLE COUNTRY.

Every Department is Crowded with New Spring Goods.

New Prints at 6½c., regular price 10c.
The most beautiful Chambray Checks for children's wear, only 15c.
Novelties in Ginghams at 10c. a yard, and a great variety of Cotton
Dress Materials.
All-Wool Serges, in twenty-five different shades, at 25c., worth 40c.
New Ottoman Cords, in all new colors, at 15c. per yard.
A great specialty with us this season in our Black Silks. We have had a
line made specially for us. They are "Wear Resisting and absolutely pure
dye." Only six prices, from 50c. to $2.50. Great value.
Great stock of Mantles and Materials ; also New Millinery and New
Trimmings.

In our Clothing Department, during the Rebellion, we are offering

Boy's Serge Suit for 98 cents.
Man's Serge Suit for $3 25.
Fine Spring Overcoat for $2.90.

OUR COLORED WORSTED RAINBOW SUIT FOR $15 !

Gentleman's White Shirt only 58c.   Gent's Regatta Shirt with Collar only 58c.

A number of our men have gone to the war, but business will go on as usual,
wit. desperate Bargains all through the house.

THOS. THOMPSON & SON,

Mammoth House, King Street East, Toronto.

C.P. MULVANEY
The North West Rebellion

Batoche will long be remembered with a shudder in too many
Canadian households. It broke the back of the rebellion, but too
many brave hearts are now cold and still that beat high with valour,
hope and noble ambition as the *Northcote's* whistle gave the signal
that the fight had begun.

Though the Indians under Big Bear continued to offer a stub-
born resistance for a time, the Half-breed rebellion as such was
crushed, and the hope of the Half-breeds was extinguished when
some of their bravest and best lay in the rifle pits that fatal Monday afternoon soaked in their own life blood. We may hate Riel,
we may abhor rebellion; but when time shall have elapsed sufficient to enable us to look at the events of this sad affair with un-
prejudiced eyes, there is not a Canadian worthy of the name who
will not remember with sincere respect and admiration Gabriel
Dumont and his valiant little band of compatriots who fought so
gallantly in their hopeless cause.

MAXIME LEPINE
(ANONYMOUSLY TRANSLATED)
Maxime Lepine's Account: Fish Creek

"I corroborate the report of Mr. Dumont up to the moment
of the departure of Mr. Riel, for Mr. Riel left it to the choice of
the people whether he was to go away or stay. The answer he
received was to go and assist the women and children. About half-
past eight in the morning I started to get something to eat at the
house of the widow Tourond, and about nine o'clock we left, Pierre
Henry, Isidore Dumas and I, to come to the coulee. Our people
made signs to us that the police were coming. Then we took up
our position to wait for them, and we had hardly taken our places
when shots were heard at the other end. As soon as we heard
the shots we rushed to that side. When we got there our people
were already all scattered and the battle had commenced. Not
long after I saw that Jerome Henry was wounded, and we then
took up a position in the coulee nearly on the bank, and I spent
nearly the whole day there. The time seemed so long that I thought
it was already evening, but on looking at my watch I saw that it
was only noon. Before noon we heard shots all around us; but
we heard shots also from the direction of Tourond's, showing that
there were still some of our people in that direction. In the afternoon we heard no more shots there, and I thought that our people on that side were all dead. Near us, and towards Mr.
Tourond's, we heard shouts, and I think it was Gabriel Dumont
and his people who were there. I know that Alec Gervais was
there, for I saw him come from that direction, and then we saw
that we were surrounded, for we saw men on all sides; we then
heard the bugle to the right of our position and we heard the
soldiers coming in the wood of the coulee, for we heard the
branches breaking, and there were others along the wood to the
left; and we heard voices speaking all around us and in front on
the prairie, and then I thought we were lost. When they came
into the wood we heard dreadful firing on every side. It was then
between three and four o'clock in the afternoon. After that they
retreated, and it seemed to me that the volleys were less fre-
quent; and about five o'clock all was quiet for a good while, only
a few sentinels seemed to be stationed at intervals watching us.
During that period we thought they were getting ready to come
and take us. After that we said to one another, 'We must try

somehow to kill one each if they come, and we must each of us fire a good shot.' And Charles Trottier counted the men there, and out of one hundred and sixty that were there at the beginning there remained but fifty-four. I do not know whether he counted the wounded. And then we consulted as to how we were to get away, and we decided to wait until night and then to run the risk of breaking our way out. But we knew that many of us must be killed in that undertaking. And then we also thought of our wounded and it seemed to me that the only assistance I could leave them was the crucifix I had held in my hand all day, but when I spoke of that no person answered me; and we were praying all that time and I had the crucifix and I said 'We shall commend ourselves to God and pray that we may have perfect contrition, so that if we die we may save our souls.' And then I prayed; for I thought we were about to die and I had doubts as to the justice of our cause. And I thought all our people were dead and that our small party were all that remained. But Delorme did me good when he said to me, 'We must pray to God to take us out of this.' And almost immediately they again commenced firing, not many rifle shots, but four cannon shots, and two or three out of the four seemed to me to burst over our heads. And all the balls seemed to fall like hail. And after these four cannon shots all became quiet, and we heard a man from among the police shout to us, speaking in the Cree tongue. He said, 'His name was Borie,' and, it seemed to me, 'that we must be hungry,' and he asked to be allowed to visit us. He also asked us to tell him how many we were. And some of the others answered him, but I do not remember what they said to him. But they would not let him come. I was inclined to let him come, and felt tempted to tell him to come, but I thought it better to say nothing for fear of making a mistake and being blamed afterwards. It occurred to me that while he was with us the police would not fire, and meantime night would set in and we should be able to get away. But almost immediately afterwards our people came up and the soldiers fled and did not fire again and we came away.

"We prayed all the day, and I think prayer did more than bullets. Often when the soldiers appeared on the hillcocks our people fired and that made them fall back and others came to remove them."

PETER HOURIE
At Batoche: Tom Hourie Rides Under Fire

"When we got to Batoche nothing could be done for three days, I think it was. Colonel Williams was fatally wounded. The General had gone down to see the river pits as well as he could, and to see how he could get at them. He took me and my son Tom with him, and some of his own men went along too. He sent one of his men right over to see if he could see any rifle pits. The poor fellow got shot dead. The General said to Tom, 'Do you think you could manage to get there, and see any of these rifle pits?' 'Yes,' Tom said. He had a pretty swift horse. He just belted right through. The half-breeds were just cooking. They ran away from their cooking right into their badger holes. Tom raced along the bank on his horse for about a mile. He raced along the front of the rifle pits on our side of the river. He was under fire. They fired at him all the time. Of course, the horse was too swift, and they could not get their shots in well.

"General Middleton laughed; we all laughed. When Tom came back, General Middleton said: 'You got a warm reception.' 'Oh, yes,' said Tom. 'I would not like to try it again.' Then we had to go back when we found where the rifle pits were. The half-breeds were in a devil of a fix. The did not know how to take it. Colonel Williams was drilling his men. I heard Colonel Williams say to the men: 'Down there we must go if not one of us returns.' Down they went right for Batoche. Here was Tom and Captain French who got shot at Batoche's house. We followed after. Then we heard shots and heard men running right across in the town; the little bit of a town. There was Billy Sinclair one of the transport men following the crowd on foot. He went into the bush for a purpose and found a rifle. He said: 'See what I've got.' I said: 'Billy let me have a spear and you can have the gun.' We ran down to the village. We were all harboured now behind the house. There was a second bank where the rifle pits were. When we got there there was a fellow just running across the street to another house. He was a soldier. He got a bullet and fell over. It was pitiful.

THE DEATH OF CAPTAIN FRENCH, OF FORT QU'APPELLE

"Then Captain French got it. Tom and Captain French got to
Batoche's house. Captain French poked his gun through the house
— through the glass. There was a fellow waiting and watching.
He fired back at the Captain's arm and the bullet went right through
his heart. Captain French said: 'Well, Tom, I'm shot, but never
mind; we were the first that came here.' He was dead just in no
time.

"Tom was out racing round from place to place, back and forth.
When we were down there the enemy all ran for it, Riel, and all
of them. The men ran from the rifle pits, but the women and children were left down there. It was a pretty steep bank and I went
strolling down there. A fellow, one of the enemy, had got shot,
whose name was Ross. A woman said to me, 'Did you see my
man?' I said: 'I saw a man lying there shot; it might be him.' She
was crying. I went along under the bank. There were the women
and children, and the women were crying to me for help. They
said the men were helping themselves to everything they could
get. Oh, it was shameful. Whatever money they got they took
it all. I went to the General and asked him to send down one of
the Captains and myself to tell the men not to disturb anything
at all, and to tell the women they would be looked after and taken
care of. By and by I got the women all up on to the bank and got
them in their tents and told them nobody should harm them —
and that was done."

CLEOMATI
To One of the Absent

You bade me good-bye with a smile, love,
   And away to the west wild and drear ;
At the sound of war's bugle shrill calling
   You went without shadow of fear.
But when I complained of your going,
   To face dangers untold in the west ;
You chided me gently by singing :
   "Encourage me dear 'twill be best."

"I know you will miss me each hour
   And grieve when I'm far, far away :
But its duty's demand and I'm ready ;
   Could I show the white feather to-day?
Oh! Now, you're my own bright eyed blessing
   And show the true spirit within :
Those eyes now so fearlessly flashing
   Shall guide me through war's crash and din."

With your men you went cheerful and willing,
   To defend and take peace to the poor
Helpless children and sad prisoned women
   Who had homes on Saskatchewan's shore,
And now I'm so proud of you darling
   I can worship a hero so brave,
While I pray for your safe home returning ;
   When the peace flag shall quietly wave.

O'er the land where poor Scott's heartless murderer,
   Has added much more to his sin ;
By the cold-blooded uncalled for slaughter,
   Of Gowanlock, Delaney and Quinn,
Who like many others now sleeping,
   Shroudless near the sky of the west,
May be called the sad victims and martyrs
   Of Riel who's name we detest.

Many hearts are now mourning their lov'd ones
　　Who died at their post, true and brave,
In defiance of one heartless rebel,
　　Who's life not e'en "millions" should save.
So keep your arm strong for the fray dear,
　　I'll not wish you back 'ere the fight
Shall decide for you, country and comrades,
　　In favour of honour and right.

Let justice be done now unfailing
　　Nought but *death* can atone for his sin ;
Let the fate he has meted to others ;
　　By our dauntless be meted to him,
Don't return until quiet contentment ;
　　Fills the homes now deserted out west,
And the true ring of peace finds an echo,
　　In each sturdy settler's breast.

And when you are homeward returning,
　　With heart that has never known fear ;
Remember the love light is burning,
　　Unceasingly, constantly, here
And "Bright Eyes" will give you a welcome
　　Which even a soldier may prize
While the lips will be smiling with pleasure,
　　That have prayed in your absence with sighs.

And the whole world shall ring with the praises
　　Of Canada's noblest and best ;
Who shoulder to shoulder defended,
　　And saved the unhappy NorthWest
While in coming years 'round the hearthstone
　　Will be told how the dark coats and red,
Put to rout Riel, rebels and half-breeds
　　And aveng'd both the living and dead.

LOUIS RIEL

Chanson de Riel

Ce'est au chantier bataille,
J'ai fait cri' mes douleurs.
Vou' est 'cun dout' surpasse,
Ca fait frémir les coeurs.

Or je r'çois t'une lettre
De ma chérie maman.
J'avais ni plum' ni encre
Pour pou(r) voir leur z'écrire.

Or je pris mon ganife,
Je le trempi dans mon sang,
Pour écrir' t'un' vieu' lettre
De ma chérie maman.

Quand ell' r'çoivra cette lettre
Tou(s) écriture en sang,
Ses yeux baignant dans larmes,
Son coeur s'en va mourant.

S'y jett' à g'noux par terre
En (ap)pelant sis enfants:
Priez pour votr' p'tit frère
Qui l'est au régiment.

Mourir, s'est pour mourir(e)
Chacun meurt à son tour;
J'aim' mieux mourir en brave,
Faut tou(s) mourir un jour.

LOUIS RIEL
(TRANSLATED BY
FATHER RUFIN TURCOTTE)

Riel Song

It is on the battle field,
I cried my pains,
You no doubt surpass yourself,
It makes the heart shudder.

So I receive a letter,
From my dear mother,
I had no feather, no ink,
To write to them.

So I take my pen knife,
I dipped it in my blood,
To write an old letter,
To my dear mother.

When she will receive this letter,
All written in blood,
Her eyes bathed in tears,
Her heart dying slowly

She throws herself on her knees,
Calling her children;
Pray your little brother,
Who is at the regiment.

To die is for dying.
Each die on his turn,
I prefer to die as a brave,
We all have to die one day.

34

GABRIEL DUMONT

WANDERING SPIRIT — THE WARRIOR

LOUIS RIEL

LOUIS RIEL
(TRANSLATED BY
BARBARA CASS-BEGGS)

Chanson de Louis Riel

Louis Riel Song

1.
C'est au champ de bataille
J'ai fait écrir' douleurs.
On couche sur la paille,
Ça fait frémir les coeurs.

1.
I send this lettre to you
To tell my grief and pain,
And as I lie imprisoned
I long to see again

2.
Or je r'çois t'une lettre
De ma chère maman.
J'avais ni plum' ni encre
Pour pouvoir lui z'écrire.

2.
You, my beloved mother,
And all my comrades dear.
I write these words in my
heart's blood:
No ink or pen is here.

3.
Or je pris mon canif,
Je le trempis dans mon sang,
Pour écrir' t'un vieu' lettre
À ma chere maman.

3.
My friends in arms and children,
Please weep and pray for me.
I fought to keep our country
So that we might be free.

4.
Quand ell' r'çevra cett' lettre
Toute écrit' de sang,
Ses yeux baignant de larmes,
Son coeur sera mourant.

4.
When you receive this letter
Please weep for me and pray
That I may die with bravery
Upon that fearful day.

5.
S'y jett' à genoux par terre
En appelant ses enfants:
Priez pour votre frère
Qui est au régiment.

6.
Mourir, s'il faut mourir,
Chacun meurt à son tour;
J'aim' mieux mourir en brave,
Faut tous mourir un jour.

LOUIS RIEL
(TRANSLATED BY JOHN GLASSCO)
From _A Sir John A. MacDonald_

Sir John A. MacDonald doth govern proudly
The provinces from which his power flows;
While his bad faith perpetuates my woes—
And all his countrymen applaud him loudly.

Despite the peace he owes me, and despite
His pledge to honour in the deed and fact
            What was our Pact[1]
            And is my right,
  For seven years now Sir John has warred with me.
  A faithless man's a vulgar man, be he
Either a wise man or a witling born :
       And so I hold him up to scorn.

He meant to cast into obscure disgrace
      The Bishop of Saint Boniface;[2]
Then finding his mistake, he made a show of
  candour
         And sought to save his face
         Before His Grace
  By bidding this good Pontiff Alexander
  Appease the Métis and their proper wrath,
  And to be sure to let them understand
         They'd followed the right path
       In taking up their own defence
       Since the vile Schultzes[3] and
       MacDougalls[4]
Had all received a rightful reprimand
For causing us, with their damned drums and
  bugles,
        Such dire alarms
        When they took arms
Against us, _sans_ authority
Of Her Most Gracious Majesty.

He played the Bishop false, and then belied
Him with fair words and with such *politesse*
      As cloaked his wickedness,
And pleased his party and his gang beside.

Despite his plots in their deceitful dress,
Despite his pride in his own cleverness,
He'll answer one day to a wrathful God
For all the injustice he hath sown abroad.
He's a fine speaker is the Parliamentary chief,
And sits among the great ones of the land;
But once Sir John's become so many grains of sand,
    God will arraign him at His Judgement Seat,
        Where he must stand.

      In eighteen hundred and seventy-three,
        With poor Lépine[5] in gaol
And Manitoba in her agony,
And I hunted man with all men on my trail,
    Sir John offered me thirty-five thousand
      dollars[6]
    If for three years I would desert my nation
        In all her dolours,
And leave my friend Lépine in tribulation,
        With bleeding feet and hands
        Captived in iron bands[7]

          *   *   *   *

   How happy was I one fine day to view
   Sir John laid low, with all his wretched
      crew![8]

But still his projects were much narrower in scope
   Than those of Edward Blake[9] and of
      MacKenzie.[10]
   When Blake closed off the future—and our
      hope—

'Twas then, in a fine frenzy,
That he announced the Price of Blood,[11]
And, bidding justice cease,
Destroyed an innocent people's livelihood
By thus condemning, in its leaders, the Métis.

Almighty God! Protect Thy poor Métis
Almost abolished by the English race...

And as for you, Sir John,
I do not wish your death should be
Too full of suffering, of course;
But what I'd like to see
Is that you should feel some remorse,
Because, you Vampire, you have eaten me.

                *   *   *   *

Canadians! The English whom you trust
Are neither generous nor just,
But quite the opposite,
Open your eyes, and be convinced of it!
Carthage ne'er boasted of her Punic faith,
Because her sons had still some self-respect.
But see the modern Englishman, erect
In all his shameless brag
Of British justice and the British flag!
Too well we see in all his actions
How he aspires, if none gainsaith,
By every means to make us Anglo-Saxons.
But Lower Canada was never born to perish
Her bishops are all ready, I believe,
To endure the loss of all they cherish,
If need be, rather than to leave
You, John, to do just as you please
Whene'er you mean to make them hold their
peace.

And the good God has given *me* strength and
   heart,
And I'll not die without declaring war,
         The war of sense and art
         And of the rights of man
         Against all that you are.
My strength is in my gift for suffering;
I am the man to leap into the ring.
         And give all that he can
         And more than John Bull reckons:
He has gored me all too often with his horn;
I'll beat him yet; and I shall have for seconds
Princess Louise and the Marquess of Lorne.

          *   *   *   *

         I laugh at those who place
         Vile flattery above
         The sacred love
A man feels for his native land and race;
And at Lord Dufferin I can laugh indeed,
That still-born child launched from old Erin's
   womb,
         Who did not come
Into the world headfirst, but by his bum.[12]

He and his wife have now re-crossed the ocean.
We saw them leave with no profound emotion...

         They've had illustrious successors
Sprung from the marquisate and royal line.
A poor and almost peasant stock is mine,
      But through it I pretend
    Unto the principality
Of moral principles, and will defend
      The Good against all bad oppressors;

And this is why
I hate a policy that's based on Vice,
And its employ
Even in a Viceroy.

The unjust man lives peacefully in his house of
    clay;
    But its foundation will collapse one day.
Be sure that Washington is closer, in our view,
Than London, and your neighbours worthier far
    than you!

If God saw fit to cut us off from France
In spite of all the bonds of our affection,
Remember also that the power she can
    advance
May in a twinkling break old Albion's
    sceptre.
            Take care:
I, I am watching you. Beware!
Your whole empire, and all those who have
    kept her
Glorious, fall apart. Too long and much too
    often
She's thrown false dice upon her mouldy
    coffin.

And all too long the children of New France
        Have borne the English yoke;
        And will not miss the chance
Of crushing a decrepit race, and so revoke
The rule of those who, in a pride not to be borne,
        Have governed them with such inveterate scorn!

[1]The amnesty promised in 1869 to all Métis involved in the Red River insurrection.

[2]Msgr Alexandre Taché, Riel's early patron.

[3]Dr. John (later Sir John) Schultz, a leading figure in the 'Canadian' party in Manitoba, and Riel's arch-enemy.

[4]Hon. William McDougall, Minister of Public Works in MacDonald's first cabinet. Appointed Lieutenant-Governor of Rupert's Land in 1869, he was ignominiously turned back at the border by an armed band of Métis.

[5]Ambrose Lépine, Riel's lieutenant throughout the insurrection of 1869-70, and president of the court martial which imposed the death sentence on Thomas Scott.

[6]This has never been confirmed.

[7]Lépine was arrested in 1873 on a charge of murder.

[8]MacDonald's government was defeated in 1873.

[9]Liberal premier of Ontario in 1871.

[10]Alexander Mackenzie, who headed a Liberal government in 1873.

[11]Blake's government offered $5000 for the apprehension of Riel and Lépine as the murderers of Scott.

[12]This reference is obscure.

LOUIS RIEL
A Prisoner's Plea

Would the governor
And the Government
Grant me a favour
In my detainment
My wife, my children
Are poor, have no bread
Could I use my pen
In Jail, for their aid.

Grant me to describe
Scenes in the North West
To write on the tribe
Which has help'd me best
Allow me to pass
Word of my morning
When I saw the mass
Of your braves winning.

Ah! perhaps, your press
And your volunteers
Would, in my distress
Buy my reading tears
I would with the price
Get for my children
Half a cup of rice
Or half a chicken.

Sing, O my verses!
Try and earn, in spite
Of my reverses
Yet a gentle bite
Some bread, for my wife,
My dear Margaret
And spare her a strife
With want and regret

Margaret! I told
You and your father
Before we enroll'd
Our lives together
That my future was
Still clouded with storms
How my career has
Come to its grand forms.

O Captain! I would
write with discretion
And carefully should
I get permission
To work out humbly
The bread that I wish
For my family
The bread of anguish.

WILLIAM WILFRED CAMPBELL
In the North-West

"FORWARD!"
        The captain said,
Out of the morning's red
Brave and noble and dread,
With hero and martial tread,
Into the North and the Westward.

Over dim forest and lake,
Over lone prairie and brake,
The clamor of battle to wake,
For kindred and country's sake,
Into the North and the Westward.

"Forward!"
        'Neath northern sky,
Ready to fight and die:
Where the shadowy marshbirds fly
With their weird and lonely cry,
Far to the North and the Westward.

Only the rifle's crack,
And answer of rifle back;
Heavy each haversack,
Dreary the prairie's track
Far to the North and the Westward.

"Forward!"
        Seeking the foe,
Starving and bleeding they go,
Into the sleet and the snow,
Over bleak rivers that flow
Far to the North and the Westward.

Falling on frozen strands;
Falling, devoted bands,
Sleeping with folded hands!
Dead, for home and for lands—
Dead in the North and the Westward!

BARRY DANE
Métis, 1885

How many buffets must the bondsman bear,
  Till in just anger he return the blow
  With a swift stroke that lays the tyrant low?
How long must he the galling fetters wear,
Till it be well that he arise and dare
  To rend and cast them, counting each his foe
  Who would subdue within his breast the glow
Of equal manhood that is kindled there?
How long a people mutely suffer wrong?
  How long be suppliant ere they make demand?
How long be spurned, till in a surging throng
  They gather, stern of purpose, strong of hand,
To throttle the oppressor of the land,
  And live immortal in their country's song?

PATRICK ANDERSON
Poem on Canada

IV *The Country Still Unpossessed*

Though Champlain looked in it for the Lilies of France
and Laval looked in it for the wounds of Christ,
and the holy sisters found its winters chaste
while the merchants, with the Hurons gliding about it,
declared it merry with flies and mad with waste:
and the Jesuit Fathers wrote of it in Relations,
sprinkling the holy water which often froze
and a boy climbed over the Quebec stockade
and stared at it too long — and it chipped his nose.

Then, chased by his wife, Frontenac bowed to it
with the silver of Montmorency in his hand,
walking in the blue water as on a parquet
swept by a foam of girls, in his native land,
with military honours to beat the band:
but the Iroquois looked in it for a priest to fry —
a string of red-hot hatchets about his neck —
while the glory of God and brandy and beads to buy
enriched the pioneer *seigneurs* of Quebec.
And the explorers found in it new trails to begin
and Wolfe stood there, and felt his receding chin.

And, despite the traders, despite the *coureurs de bois*
and the *voyageurs*, and those who slung canals
and fastened bridges above them, or sharpened their dreams
to the wizened and hungry winter of the rails
westward, forever — or fenced and festooned the miles,
this Laurentide land, boosted with waterpower
and blown from the North, was greater and grander by far.

There, grimy with toil, the lightning dipped like a miner
to dig in the precious ores with a pointed flash
while high in their secret mountains the magnet lakes
drew shining up their loyalties of fish.

And despite the fever in land or timber or wheat,
the country remained, and the people looked into it.

And Mackenzie looked in it for electoral rights
and the popular will, but all that he could see
was Governor Head who was quite prepared to fight
"the low-bred antagonist democracy" —
"I would publicly promulgate, let them come if they dare!"
the Governor said (a man with important curls,
with a scheming brain but a fine crisp head of hair
and tight thin lips and eyes that glazed like pearls).
Mackenzie, five times elected and five denied,
prepared to fight it out, appealed to the South,
and smiling "wiped his seditious little mouth" —
blood ran in Toronto's snow and the people died.

And Papineau looked in it for the popular will
and was beaten back: with trumpets Lord Durham came
and saw division and graft, dissension and spoil,
and wrote his notes and left, a dying man:
and in it looked the Fathers of Confederation,
profits and "progress" all that they could know —
the bourgeois midwives of a new-born nation —
from cold colony to empty dominion, so —
yet laid the ground where greater changes grow.

And Riel, not mad. *Pas fou*. At his own trial
forsook what his lawyers said and madness forever
and claimed the great dignity of the conscious will
for what he had said and done on the Red River
for freedom and the Métis. Gave up his right
to pardon. Was ordered hanged as a traitor.
But they said his body made a great wound in the air
and God damn the English judge that put him there!

And Laurier looked at it, in the time of war,
and thought of a national future, and died before.

And the factories built. And the companies seizing the forests,
the companies burning wheat in the prairie dust,
the fortunes solemn as coal or gaudy as water
while the Regina dead were specks in the Golden West,
only by hunger published and soon dismissed.
But the unions formed. The gradual moulding of labour
in crisis and slump, the logic that hunger inspired —
while over their heads the land was wavy with leisure
though lakes were shining days as yet unexplored.

LOUIS RIEL

E.J. PRATT
Hollow Echoes from the Treasury Vault

Sir John was tired as to the point of death.
His chin was anchored to his chest. Was Blake
Right after all? And was Mackenzie right?
Superior could be travelled on. Besides,
It had a bottom, but those northern bogs
Like quicksands could go down to the earth's core.
Compared with them, quagmires of ancient legend
Were backyard puddles for old ducks. To sink
Those added millions down that wallowing hole!
He thought now through his feet. Many a time
When argument cemented opposition,
And hopeless seemed his case, he could think up
A tale to laugh the benches to accord.
No one knew better, when a point had failed
The brain, how to divert it through the ribs.
But now his stock of stories had run out.
This was exhaustion at its coma level.
Or was he sick? Never had spots like these
Assailed his eyes. He could not rub them out—

Those shifting images—was it the sunset
Refracted through the bevelled window edges?
He shambled over and drew down the blind;
Returned and slumped; it was no use; the spots
Were there. No light could ever shoot this kind
Of orange through a prism, or this blue.

And what a green! The spectrum was ruled out;
Its bands were too inviolate. He rubbed
The lids again—a brilliant gold appeared
Upon a silken backdrop of pure white,
And in the centre, red—a scarlet red,
A dancing, rampant and rebellious red
That like a stain spread outward covering
The vision field. He closed his eyes and listened:
Why, what was that? 'Twas bad enough that light
Should play such pranks upon him, but must sound
Crash the Satanic game, reverberate
A shot fifteen years after it was fired,
And culminate its echoes with the thud
Of marching choruses outside his window:

"We'll hang Riel up the Red River,
And he'll roast in hell forever,
We'll hang him up the River
With a yah-yah-yah."

The noose was for the shot; 'twas blood for blood;
The death of Riel for the death of Scott.
What could not Blake do with that on the Floor,
Or that young, tall, bilingual advocate
Who with the carriage of his syllables
Could bid an audience like an orchestra
Answer his body swaying like a reed?
Colours and sounds made riot of his mind—
White horses in July processional prance,
The blackrobe's swish, the Métis' sullen tread,
And out there in the rear the treaty-wise
Full-breeds with buffalo wallows on their foreheads.

This he could stand no longer, sick indeed:
Send for his doctor, the first thought, then No;
The doctor would advise an oculist,
The oculist return him to the doctor,
The doctor would see-saw him to another—
A specialist on tumours of the brain,
And he might recommend close-guarded rest
In some asylum—Devil take them all,
He had his work to do. He glanced about
And spied his medicine upon the sideboard;
Amber it was, distilled from Highland springs,
That often had translated age to youth
And boiled his blood on a victorious rostrum.
Conviction seized him as he stood, for here
At least he was not cut for compromise,
Nor curried to his nickname Old Tomorrow.
Deliberation in his open stance,
He trenched a deep one, gurgled and sat down.
What were those paltry millions after all?
They stood between completion of the Road
And bankruptcy of both Road and Nation.
Those north-shore gaps must be closed in by steel.
It did not need exhilarated judgment
To see the sense of that. To send the men
Hop-skip-and-jump upon lake ice to board
The flatcars was a revelry for imps.
And all that cutting through the mountain rock,
Four years of it and more, and all for nothing,
Unless those gaps were spanned, bedded and railed.

To quit the Road, to have the Union broken
Was irredeemable. He rose, this time
Invincibility carved on his features,
Hoisted a second, then drew up the blind.
He never saw a sunset just like this.
He lingered in the posture of devotion:
That sun for sure was in the west, or was it?
Soon it would be upholstering the clouds
Upon the Prairies, Rockies and the Coast:
He turned and sailed back under double-reef.
Cabined himself inside an armchair, stretched
His legs to their full length under the table.
Something miraculous had changed the air—
A chemistry that knew how to extract
The iron from the will: the spots had vanished
And in their place an unterrestrial nimbus
Circled his hair: the jerks had left his nerves:
The millions kept on shrinking or were running
From right to left: the fourth arthritic digit
Was straight, and yes, by heaven, the little fifth
Which up to now was just a calcium hook
Was suppling in the Hebridean warmth.
A blessèd peace fell like a dew upon him,
And soon, in trance, drenched in conciliation,
He hiccuped gently—"Now let S-S-Stephen come!"

*(The Government grants the Directors the right to issue $35,000,000, guarantees
$20,000,000, the rest to be issued by the Railway Directors. Stephen goes to London,
and Lord Revelstoke, speaking for the House of Baring, takes over the issue.)*

RAYMOND SOUSTER
Riel, 16 novembre, 1885

"Rome is fallen": Riel,
rousing the Métis for the last time.

He walked at Batoche
among the rifle pits
carrying a crucifix,
hoping for a miracle.

But never a gun.
"I do not like war."

Always beware the leader
who talks with God
and leaves you to do the dirty work.

JOHN ROBERT COLOMBO
The Last Words of Louis Riel

Your Honours, Gentlemen of the Jury: You have seen
that I am naturally inclined to think of God
at the beginning of my actions. If I do it now,
I wish you won't take it as a mark of insanity,
that you won't take it as part of a play of insanity.

Oh my God! help me through thy grace
and the divine influence of Jesus Christ.
Oh my God! bless me, bless me, bless this Honourable Court,
bless this Honourable Jury, bless my good lawyers
who have come seven hundred leagues to try to save my life,
bless also the lawyers for the Crown,
because they have done, I am sure,
what they thought their duty.
They have shown me fairness which at first
I did not expect of them.

Oh my God! bless all those who are around me,
through the grace and influence of Jesus Christ Our Saviour,
change the curiosity of those who are paying attention to me,
change that curiosity into sympathy for me.

The day of my birth I was helpless
and my mother took care of me
although she was not able to do it alone,
there was someone to help her to take care of me and I lived.
Today, although a man, I am helpless before this Court,
in the Dominion of Canada and in this world,
as I was helpless on the knees of my mother the day of my birth.
The North-West is also my mother, it is my mother country.

Although my mother country is sick and confined in a certain way,
there are some from Lower Canada who came to help her
to take care of me during her sickness,
and I am sure that my mother country will not kill me
more than my mother did forty years ago,
when I came into the world,
because a mother is always a mother,
and even if I have my faults, if she can see I am true,
she will be full of love for me.

When I came into the North-West in July of 1884,
I found the Indians suffering, I found
the Half-breeds eating the rotten pork of the Hudson Bay Company,
and getting sick and weak every day...
I also paid attention to them,
I saw they were deprived of responsible Government.
I saw they were deprived of their public liberties.
I remembered that the greatest part of my heart and blood was white,
and I have directed my attention to help the Indians
to help the Half-breeds and to help the whites
to the best of my ability. We have made petitions,
I have made petitions, with others, to the Canadian Government,
asking to relieve the condition of this country.
We have taken time, we have tried to unite
all classes, even if I may so speak, all parties.
Those who have been in close communication with me
know I have suffered, that I have waited months
to bring some of the people of the Saskatchewan
to an understanding of certain important points in our petitions
to the Canadian Government, and I have done my duty.
No one can say that the North-West has not suffered,
particularly the Saskatchewan; for the other parts
of the North-West I cannot say so much,
but what I have done and risked I had to do,
was called upon to do something for my country.

It is true I believed for years that I had a mission,
I believe at this very moment I had a mission.
What encourages me to speak to you with more confidence,
in all the imperfections of my English way of speaking,
is that I have yet and still that mission,
and with the help of God, who is in this box with me —
and he is on the side of my lawyers,
even with the Honourable Court, the Crown and the jury —
to help me and to prove by the extraordinary help
that there is a Providence today in my trial
as there was a Providence in the battles of the Saskatchewan.

I say that I have been blessed by God
and I hope that you will not take that
as a presumptuous assertion. It has been a great success
for me to come through all the dangers
I have in the last fifteen years.
If I have not succeeded in wearing a fine coat myself
I have at the same time the great consolation
of seing that God has maintained my views;
that he has maintained my health sufficiently
to go through the world
and that he has kept me from bullets
when bullets marked my hat. I am blessed by God.

I say that we have been patient a long time
and when we see that mild words
only serve as covers for great ones to do wrong,
it is time when we are justified in saying
that robbery is robbery everywhere,
and the guilty ones are bound by the force of public opinion
to take notice of it.
The one who has the courage to speak out in that way
instead of being an outrageous man becomes in fact
a benefactor to those men themselves, and to society.

Yes, I said there will be trouble in the North-West
and was it so or not? Has there been no trouble in the North-West?
Besides, the Half-breeds as hunters can foretell many things,
perhaps some of you have a special knowledge of it.
I have seen Half-breeds who say: "My hand is shaking,
this part of my body is shaking, you will see such a thing today,"
and it happens. Others will say: "I feel the flesh of my leg
move in such a way, it is a sign of such a thing,"
and it happens. There are men who know that I speak right.

I am no more than you are. I am simply one of the flock,
equal to the rest. If it is any satisfaction to the doctor
to know what kind of insanity I have, if they are going
to call my pretentions insanity, I say, humbly,
through the grace of God,
I believe I am the prophet of the New World.

We took up arms against the invaders from the East
without knowing them. They were so far apart from us,
on the other side of the Lakes, that it cannot be said
that we had any hatred against them. We did not know them.
They came without notification. They came boldly. We said:
"Who are they?" They said: "We are the possessors of the country."
Well, knowing that it was not true, we did against those parties
coming from the East what we did against the Indians
from the South and from the West, when they would invade us.
Public opinion in the States helped us a great deal...besides,
the Opposition in Canada did the same thing and said to the
    Government:
"Well, why did you go into the North-West without consulting
    the people?"
We took up arms, we made hundreds of prisoners, and we negotiated.
A treaty was made. The treaty was made by a delegation of both parties.
Whether you consider the organization of the Red River people
at that time as a Provisional Government or not,
the fact is that we were recognized as a body,
tribal, if you like to call it so, as a social body
with whom the Canadian Government treated.

Do you own the lands? In England, in France, the French
and the English have land, the first who were in England,
they were the owners of the soil and they transmitted it to generations.
Now by the soil they have had their start as a nation.
Who starts the nations? The very same one who creates them,
God.
God is the master of the universe, our planet is his land,
and the nations, the tribes, are members of his family,
and as a good Father he gives a portion of his lands to that nation,
to that tribe, to everyone, that is his heritage, that is his share
of the inheritance, of the people, or nation, or tribe.
Now here is a nation, strong as it may be,
it has had its inheritance from God, when they have crowded
their country because they have no room to stay at home,
it does not give them the right to come and take the share
of the small tribe beside them, when they come they ought to say:
"Well, my little sister, the Cree tribe,
you have a great territory, but that territory
has been given to you as your own land,
has been given to our fathers in England,
or in France, and of course you cannot exist
without having that spot of land."
This is the principle. God cannot create a tribe
without locating it, we are not birds,
we have to walk on the ground.

It is to be understood that there were
two societies who treated together.
One was small, but in its smallness it had its rights.
The other was great, but in its greatness it had no greater rights
than the rights of the small, because the right is
the same for every one, and when they began by treating the leaders
of that small community as bandits, as outlaws,
leaving them without protection,
they disorganized that community.

I will speak of the wish of my heart.
I have been asserted to be wrong today,
I hope that before long that very same thing
which was said wrong will be known as good...
I say my heart will never abandon
the idea of having a new island in the North-West,
by constitutional means,
inviting the Irish of the other side of the sea
to come and have a share here;
a new Poland in the North-West, by the same way;
a new Bavaria, in the same way;
a new Italy in the same way.
I want French-Canadians to come
and help us here today,
tomorrow,
I don't know when.
On the other side of the mountain
there are Indians, and Half-breeds,
and there is a beautiful island Vancouver,
and I think the Belgians will be happy there
and the Jews who are looking for a country
for eighteen hundred years,
will they perhaps hear my voice one day;
on the other side of the mountains
while the waves of the Pacific will chant
sweet music for them to console their hearts
for the mourning of eighteen hundred years,
will they perhaps say: "He is the one thought of us
in the whole Cree world"?
The Scandinavians, if possible, they will have a share.
It is my plan, it is one of the illusions of my insanity,
if I am insane, that they should have on the other side
of the mountain a new Norway,
a new Denmark and a new Sweden.

My thoughts are for peace.
But such a great revolution will bring immense disasters
and I don't want to bring disasters during my life
except those that I am bound to bring to defend my own life
and to avoid, to take away from my country, disasters
which threaten me and my friends and those who have confidence
in me. Of course they gave a chance to Riel to come out,
a rebel had a chance to be loyal then.
But with the immense influence that my acts are gathering
for the last fifteen years and which,
as the power of steam contained in an engine
will have its way, then what will I do?
I may be declared insane
because I seek such an idea,
which drives me to something right.

This was told to me.
It was also told me that men would stay in the *belle prairie*,
and the spirit spoke of those who would remain on the *belle prairie*,
and there were men who remained on the *belle prairie*.
If they declare me insane, I have been astray.
I have been astray not as an imposter,
but according to my conscience. Your Honour,
this is what I have to say.

JOHN NEWLOVE
Ride Off Any Horizon

Ride off any horizon
and let the measure fall
where it may—

on the hot wheat,
on the dark yellow fields
of wild mustard, the fields

of bad farmers, on the river,
on the dirty river full
of boys and on the throbbing

powerhouse and the low dam
of cheap cement and rocks
boiling with white water,

and on the cows and their powerful
bulls, the heavy tracks
filling with liquid at the edge

of the narrow prairie
river running steadily away.

*

Ride off any horizon
and let the measure fall
where it may—

among the piles of bones
that dot the prairie

in vision and history
(the buffalo and deer,

dead indians, dead settlers,
the frames of lost houses

left behind in the dust
of the depression,

dry and profound, that
will come again in the land

and in the spirit, the land
shifting and the minds

blown dry and empty—
I have not seen it! except

in pictures and talk—
but there is the fence

covered with dust, laden,
the wrecked house stupidly empty)—

here is a picture for your wallet,
of the beaten farmer and his wife
leaning toward each other—

sadly smiling, and emptied of desire.

*

Ride off any horizon
and let the measure fall
where it may—

off the edge
of the black prairie

as you thought you could fall,
a boy at sunset

not watching the sun
set but watching the black earth,

never-ending they said in school,
round: but you saw it ending,

finished, definite, precise—
visible only miles away.

*

Ride off any horizon
and let the measure fall
where it may—

on a hot night the town
is in the streets—

the boys and girls
are practising against

each other, the men
talk and eye the girls—

the women talk and
eye each other, the indians
play pool: eye on the ball.

*

Ride off any horizon
and let the measure fall
where it may—

and damn the troops, the horsemen
are wheeling in the sunshine,
the cree, practising

for their deaths: mr poundmaker,
gentle sweet mr bigbear,
it is not unfortunately

quite enough to be innocent,
it is not enough merely
not to offend—

at times to be born
is enough, to be
in the way is too much—

some colonel otter, some
major-general middleton will
get you, you—

indian. It is no good to say,
I would rather die
at once than be in that place—

though you love that land more,
you will go where they take you.

*

Ride off any horizon
and let the measure fall—

where it may;
it doesn't have to be

the prairie. It could be
the cold soul of the cities
blown empty by commerce

and desiring commerce
to fill up the loneliness.

The streets are full of people.

It is night, the lights
are on; the wind

blows as far as it may. The streets
are dark and full of people.

Their eyes are fixed as far as
they can see beyond each other—

to the concrete horizon, definite,
tall against the mountains,
stopping vision visibly.

R.G. EVERSON
The Métis

Canada's countrymen
killed off by their fellow citizens
invented the Red River cart
which war-whooped for nearly a century

The Métis
world champion plainsman
world champion paddler
heir of Molière's France and the Stone Age

The Métis founded two countries
and fought two wars against Canada

The Métis
of Qu'Appelle
Touchwood
Cypress Hills
Sweetgrass
Bearpaw
Wood Mountain
Little Rockies

A murdered culture

I knew the last of the Batoche Métis
dying in Montréal
Perspective turned around for the old man
as in a Grandma Moses far came near
Again the South Saskatchewan river flared
when the Winnipeg Field Battery opened fire

More die than people when an ancient dies
and tethered years wrench loose
None now can feel the Métis side of the day
at long-ago Batoche
dull anger's taste
or how the maned ungentled prairie tossed

SHIELD OF PEACE

ON RIEL

JOHN NEWLOVE
Crazy Riel

Time to write a poem
or something.
Fill up a page.
The creature noise.
Huge massed forces of men
hating each other.
What young men do not know.
To keep quiet,
contemporaneously.
Contempt. The robin diligently
on the lawn sucks up worms,
hopping from one to another.
Youthfully. Sixteen miles
from my boyhood home
the frogs sit in the grassy marsh
that looks like a golf course
by the lake. Green frogs.
Boys catch them for bait or sale.
Or caught them. Time.
To fill up a page.
To fill up a hole.
To make things feel better. Noise.
The noise of the images
that are people I will never understand.
Admire them though I may.
Poundmaker. Big Bear. Wandering Spirit,
those miserable men.
Riel. Crazy Riel. Riel hanged.
Politics must have its way.
The way of noise. To fill up.
The definitions bullets make,
and field guns.

The noise your dying makes,
to which you are the only listener.
The noise the frogs hesitate
to make as the metal hook
breaks through the skin
and slides smoothly into place
in the jaw. The noise
the fish makes caught in the jaw,
which is only an operation
of the body and the element,
which a stone would make
thrown in the same water, thrashing,
not its voice.
The lake is not displaced,
having one less jackfish body.
In the slough that looks like a golf course
the family of frogs sings. Metal throats.
The images of death hang upside-down.
Grey music.
It is only the listening for death,
fingering the paraphernalia,
the noise of the men you admire.
And cannot understand.
Knowing little enough about them.
The knowledge waxing.
The wax that paves hell's road,
slippery as the road to heaven.
So that as a man slips
he might as easily slide
into being a saint as destroyer.
In his ears the noise magnifies.
He forgets men.

R.G. EVERSON
Riding North Toward Duck Lake, Sask.

We livestock are packed loosely in the bus.
The two Indians have taken separate seats,
Papa sprawled in the right front, smaller
son beyond him, both staring ahead
enormously uninterested in anything,
for there is not a horse in sight.

From fossils, there were horses here
some sixty million years ago—went out
with the ice ages. Spanish conquistadors
returned the horses, now again scarce.

A century ago at Duck Lake
these Indians were world-class cavalry.

The bus is running into scrub-brush country
when, suddenly, a neigh of horses,
reddish manes and tails are flowing
across the road, stopping traffic, starting
both Indians crowding forward in the aisle,
yelling. Their cavalry has returned.

DON GUTTERIDGE
Riel

There is no
eloquence to
blood running
from the mouths
of wounds and
battles lost,
the eyes
of the dead
at Duck Lake
and Batoche are
white stones
darkening
           at
              the
                  centre.

I hear
no story
of their suffering
no rhythm
of waters running
blue St. Lawrence
breathing tides
the earth-red
of my own river
blending
to seed of lakes
the world
may wait
a hundred suns
to see

When my body
swings like a
dead tongue
from the white-man's
scaffolding,
will there be
an eloquence
to tell...

or will this
prairie be
a coffin
for my voice
a dwelling place
for
    two
        white
            stones?

DOROTHY LIVESAY
Prophet of the New World: A Poem for Voices

CHORUS:

Who is he that comes, treading on hope
Indian footed? Remembering how
when the lean rock pulls winter on its face
natives of the plains know time is near
to hunt the buffalo for hides, for meat
and in thin bush to trap the beaver skin?

Who is he with Ireland in his name
and Scandinavian humour in his veins?
What poet, or what dreamer, caught
in music of his own imagining?
Who is he devout and filial
with the French vowels on his tongue
l'amour de dieu within his heart:

Who is he that comes?

MADAME RIEL:

He is my son. Louis Riel, my son.
His father came from ribboned country, where
the farms run neck and neck to reach the river.
Then he came west, to find the prairie land,
Assiniboia, ruled by Hudson Bay.
He saw good earth and tilled it, built a mill
for Métis and for Indians, hunters of buffalo,
to learn new ways and settle down: *la terre*!
as did those others, white men, a colony
against lean times: the days of drought
the shrill descent of locusts.

Close to the hearth the family warmed our hearts—
Our boy grew strong: a hunter, yet a dreamer.
And bolder grew his questions, till we had
no knowledge left to give him. So we sent him east
to converse with the priests, perhaps to be

76

a son of theirs, not ours—
Until one day, my good man's life went out.
I was alone with children still to raise. The crops!
The sheep and cattle dying.
A letter sent to Montreal struck the boy's heart.
He would come home, forget about book learning—
what did *that* matter, if his people called?
He would come home.

LOUIS RIEL:

I dreamed two dreams.
Once, as a child, out on my father's riverbank
tending the sheep.
Huddled close, their woolly dumbness sensed
the wind was whistling for October. Beast to beast
they looked towards each other for a place to turn
but all being faint of heart, stayed close.
Then I grew cold, and crouched among them
my head shoved down between their warming fleece;
my heart
seemed to be beating in slow time with theirs
under the wind, in the brittle grass.

And then—
O then I heard my name called out aloud!
I raised my eyes and saw day brighten
like a sword—
till all the air was stinging with white light.

"The sheep are leaderless" my own voice spoke.

"The sheep have chosen you," another cried:
for you are *Exovede—from the flock*!
One of them! Without authority except through them.
From the flock you must go out, there where my children are
as speechmaker and peacemaker; you must be voice
for them, for Me."

I looked, but saw no thing.
Only the first snow, whirling down.
Then darkness came.
I woke, my body stiff
from huddling with the sheep.

First, I was cold; and then,
hearing The Voice, in my mind,
I was become on fire!
Afterwards the farm, its ways, its work
enfolded me. I dropped down into sleep.
I was a child again.

MADAME RIEL:

Then came the years you went away to school
to be a priest, we hoped...
Then, was it not, you dreamed
your second dream, my son?

RIEL:

I dreamed we wrestled in a wood—my Lord
with flaming tomahawk, his mind afire
and I slow animal with limbs of man
battling the light. I, crying to be known
by him, delivering fierce blows for truth
to shake my chains in helplessness—
I, pitted small against his towering
saw his blood spurt and bruises burst like flowers:
downfallen to the earth his armour lay.

Then cried out in my pity: "Lord, forgive."
And as I stooped, he was a-sudden over me
his feathers fire, his body like a blade
and I it was who bruised and streaming lay
and woke up knocking at my breast and bone...
a lonely man, but truth unfettering me!
Here on this earth to fight for freedom's light,
here in this flowered land to end the hate.

MADAME RIEL:

So. So must it be…Tell no one, son.
They'll call you mad, for sure.
Tell no one of your dream.

CHORUS:

Full of foreboding and dark; from the dark we come
suffer a little; and into the dark go.
A door closes; a sign is up, For Sale;
the hand loved garden is smothered over with weeds
daffodils plunge wilder into the wild wood
earth quickly erases where human footprint trod
and the will of man becomes but the wind's way.

Shall it all go back, return?
Earth to her ancient privilege,
city to ash, the future skyscrapers
choked in a desperate struggle for air?
Shall the plane crash, and the sky fall
and the heart that beat so wildly be muffled
its meaning merged into the massing dark?

RIEL:

Mad, did she say mad? Madness is
the meat of poetry; and every poet's mad
who has a message burning in his bowels.
Say I am mad; say that the slowly turning world
rifled with hate, red skin against white
fathers perverting sons, and all of nature made
into a kitchen midden for man's wasteful heart—
call these things *sane?* and their existence, *bliss?*
Still I am mad, who would destroy and burn
the shame of racial hate; I, the half-caste
neither white nor brown, am therefore mad:
more human, less possessed of bigotry

nearer, I feel, to the great God who came
to be amongst us, flesh, to feel
the animal passions of this creature, man.
Make me more mad, dear Father! that beyond
the barriers of everyday, my Soul
may plunge; and so, forever be on fire
a comet flashing faith upon the world.

MADAME RIEL:

So, he returned to us; to Winnipeg.
Eighteen hundred and sixty-nine
he fought the fight—
gave to the untitled, the squatters
land that the Hudson's Bay
had held for Company spoils—
"a skin for a skin" their motto.
Our Louis ripped off the "HBC"
from the Company's flag
and let the good nuns of St. Boniface
sew, in its place, the one word, "Nation."
Together we created
the Provisional Government
of Assiniboia
and in eighteen hundred and seventy-three
elected Louis Riel as our representative
to Parliament at Ottawa!
But instead of being allowed to take his seat
he, my son
was charged with the killing of Thomas Scott
by a firing squad, at Fort Garry.
The rights and wrongs of *that*
will be argued for many a year...
But Louis Riel escaped by boat down the river
and fled across the border—
officially at Ottawa they said
"banished from his own country."

RIEL:

Even an exile must keep busy, work,
forget to dream. I swept aside
all purpose other than to follow on
the turn of seasons: and to shield with love
my little ones—my wife and little ones.

MADAME RIEL:

Then, the eighteen eighties; news abroad
talk coming from the north, of hunger
and starvation in Saskatchewan;
infringement of the rights
of Métis and of Frenchmen; the native-born
and newcome pioneer both restless grown
at the indifference of the Government.

RIEL:

It came by word of mouth, an endless chain
of words, from farm to farm—
until one day dust clogged our narrow road
and clopping horses drowned the sparrow's chirp.
Two horsemen galloped up, alighted at my door—
men of brownish skin and straight brown hair
their faces known to me in dreams—
two messengers from Métis friends
calling me home across the line, to give
my wit and wisdom to their cause;
asking for aid as leader of their flock:
I, Exovede—*from their flock*! Because I knew
with my experience, how to speak well
the tongue of governments; how to set forth our rights
yet offer, still in peace, the other cheek.

I listened. Then I prayed.
And then I came.
Back to the heartland that had nourished me.

CHORUS:

What particular dream, what sad report
from the country across the chasm
does he bring, the stranger—
he whom we had almost forgotten?

Has he a name still, has he dyed his hair
or is he still exuberant and bold
and what is his news, what manner of wonders
will he propound? Will he confound us?

Look, he has changed his clothes
altered his manner of speaking:
in his gait he limps, he walks with an arm uplifted.
Is he therefore still one of us? Can he be called ours?
And do we want him?

O there is the nub of the question!
Will he hold us, spurning, until he has told all
until silence spreads like early sunlight
over and into the grass, through the wood's crannies
under the leaves, under the tight skin?

Hush. He is mounting the rostrum:
be silent, stop questioning, hold yourselves ready.
Hush, for his lips are open. His words hurl truth.

RIEL:

Le Canada pour les Canadiens!
And who are we, Canadians?
This land is mother to me,
Blood and bone.
Yet like a mother, she has room
for more. Her arms, Red River and Assiniboine,
her arms are empty. The knotty land upthrust,
charred trunk, naked torso of rock

no eyes for sight, no face
shining out of the night—
day, a deep yawn where voice should be—
pure physical, girded with rivers,
boundaried by birds,
mapped by the grooves of buffalo and wolf.
Behold my land! a stride of seven leagues,
a giant pulse! And yet no head,
no tower for the mind.

Therefore she must be peopled.
With French blood, and with the Irish
Scandinavian, Scotch.
Some German stock I'd have—Bavarians, Russians, Poles
and the lone Jew whose face is veiled
with all the mourning of these
eighteen hundred years. Perhaps for him
the waves of the Pacific will chant a sweet
slow music to console his heart.

And what of us?
We Métis rooted here
The firstfruits of the country?
Must we go backward, yield, be dispossessed?
Ah no! Not if our temper's yet
what in the past it's been. Remember 1869!
To us who share all willingly with all who come,
to us must come fair share.
I see myself The Prophet of the New World!
The land *was* ours; it shall be
ours and yours.

CHORUS:

Now all is past. The trial
the final passionate
self-defence. The hanging
at Regina.
November 1885 is history.

MADAME RIEL:

We brought his body back to Winnipeg
in a plain wooden box—
then gave him a new coffin
decent burial
in his own earth, at St. Vital.

CHORUS:

Now the dark plunge of the year is done:
we make new prophecies
and stand, unhelmeted
facing remote certainties.
In the mind's eye bare branch
leaps with encircling green—
the pushing, probing blades.
These will be here, come bomb
or barbs of love lost, lost; come fire
to hospital, museum, home.
Over a burnt black sod the grasses grow,
the vine creeps back over the shattered porch:
the ships we built, the mills, the sprawling towns
these our own hands destroy. But not
O never will the grasping claw
reach down, break earth, tear seed from seed!
and never will the child in war, the womb in woman be
made devastate. For green returns
tenacious signal, friend to ambushed eyes.

AL PURDY
The Battlefield at Batoche

Over the earthworks among slim cottonwood trees
wind whistles a wind tune
I think it has nothing to do with living or dead men
or the price of groceries
it is only wind
And walking in the wooded dish-shaped hollow
that served to protect generals and staff
officers from sniper fire
I hear a different kind of murmur
— no more than that at least not definitely
the sort of thing you do hear
every now and then in a city never
questioning because it's so ordinary
but not so ordinary here
I ask my wife "Do you hear anything?"
She smiles "Your imagination again?"
"All right then don't you wish you had one?"
"If I did I'd burn your supper..."
the sort of thing she says to annoy me
the unanswerable kind of remark
that needs time to think about
I take my time watching the green curve
of the South Saskatchewan River below
a man riding an inch-long machine a mile distant
that makes dark waves cutting the yellow wheat
I wonder if Gunner Phillips heard the sound
on the day of May 12 in 1885
before the bullet knocked him down
the stairs he spent twenty years climbing?
Did Letendre with his muzzle-loader
clamped under one arm stuffing gun powder
down the barrel and jamming in a bullet
stop remembering great itchy beasts
pushing against log palisades at night
and running the buffalo at Grand Coteau

the Sioux screaming insults from a safe distance
at men from the White Horse Plain?
— all this in dream pantomime
with that sound and nothing else?
And old Ouellette age 90
his hearing almost gone anyway
wiping off river mist from his rifle
listening — ?
Under my feet grass makes small noises
a bright-eyed creature I can't identify
is curious about me
and chitters because it's August
In May the annoyed general eats his lunch
on the cliffs ordering "a reconnaissance in force"
his officers misinterpret as "attack in force"
Midlanders   Winnipeg Rifles   Grenadiers
move out from their own positions
and burst into the Métis rifle pits
with Captain Howard from Connecticut
a demonstrator for the Colt Firearms Company
of Hartford demonstrating
death at 500 rounds a minute
with the borrowed Gatling gun
But it wasn't the sound I hear now
not the dead shifting positions underground
to dodge bullets stopped in mid-earth
here a little way under the black soil
where wheat yellow as a girl's hair blossoms
the Métis nation was born and died
as the last buffalo stumbles to his knees
and felt cold briefly while his great wool
blanket was ripped from bloody shoulders
It is for Parenteau and Desjarlais
Ah-si-we-in of the Woods Crees
for Laframboise and old Ouellette

and dark girls left alone
that such words as mine are spoken
and perhaps also for Gunner Phillips
in his grave above the South Saskatchewan
but most for myself
And I say to my wife, "Do you hear nothing?"
"I hear the poem you're writing" she says
"I knew you were going to say that" I say
In evening listening
to the duplicate rain-sound on the roof
of our camped trailer it seems
that I was wrong about my motives
and the dark girls mourning at Batoche
the dead men in shallow rifle pits
these mean something
the rain speaks to them
the seasons pass
just outside their hearing
but what they died for has faded away
and become something quite different
past justice and injustice
beyond old Ouellette and his youngest grandson
with the larking dog chasing a rabbit
green grass growing
rain falling
on the road cars passing by
Like the child I am/was I say "Me too"
camped on the battlefield of Batoche
just slightly visible in August
me an extension of anything that ever happened
a shadow behind the future
the bullets aimed at me
by Gunner Phillips and old man Ouellette
eighty-five years ago
whispering across the fields of eternity

JOHN ROBERT COLOMBO
Louis Riel
after Miroslav Holub

Children, when was
Louis Riel born,
asks the teacher.
A thousand years ago, the children answer.
A hundred years ago, the children answer.
Last year, the children answer.
No one knows.

Children, what did
Louis Riel do,
asks the teacher.

Won a war, the children answer.
Lost a war, the children answer.
No one knows.

Our neighbour had a dog
called Louis,
replies one of the children.
Our neighbour used to beat him up
and the dog died of hunger
a year ago.

Now all the children feel sorry
for Louis

GEORGE WOODCOCK
On Completing a Life of Dumont

A year I have lived in the most of my mind with you,
Acting your deeds as best I can, thinking your thoughts, and
Now I stand back, take your dark presence in my view,
And realize that though we say goodbye, easy hand
In hand, like companions ending a long hard journey,
We are still strangers, you from your world where
Violence is what happens in the natural daily way
Between animals and between men, I from the rare
Interlude of a time where peace has been a fragile
Possibility in a few favoured places for a few.
But what is the echo I hear compellingly ring
In my ear as you bow sardonically into your defile
Of dark death? What does it tell me I share with you?
Is it, fierce stranger, that freedom is a word our hearts both sing?

MICK BURRS
Under the White Hood

1. PILE OF BONES

These wounds want to be healed.
They have always wanted
to be healed.

We walk beside the creek
where the buffalo bones were heaped.
We wear dark glasses to hood our eyes.

Oil streaks the water.
Blood streaks the grass.
We pretend there are no wounds.

2. THE PLATFORM

The man approaches you in the chill air.
His boots creak on the planks.
Your hands are tied behind your back.

He places a white cotton hood
over your head — after knotting
the noose around your neck.

Now the air you breathe
is warm, your own. Your eyes
vanish behind this mask of snow.

Because your face cannot be seen
nothing is conveyed: your lips,
their silent prayer, the forgiveness

in what they say. But the man's breath
turns hot against your hooded head
before he steps away:

Louis Riel,
do you know me?
You cannot escape from me today.

3. THE LANDSCAPE

No, you cannot recall that face.
And that voice is faceless now.
His eyes have been blanked out

by the prairie snowscape
he places upon your head
instead of a crown of thorns.

All voices have become whispers
in your final, muted storm.
The snow separates their bodies

from your vision. They fear
gazing at eyes that see thru darkness.
They are all shadows, nothing more.

And the hangman, how long
has his shadow been waiting
to drape your head in snow?

4. RED RIVER

Has his ghost returned to haunt you?
The bite of a dog in that voice.
You buggers do not *dare* to shoot me!

Again he cries out from the snow
his disbelief, a white cotton bandage
covering his eyes.

You stand near the blue shadows
of your rifle-holding, buffalo-
coated men, outside the walls

of Fort Garry. The tribunal's
judgment of the night before:
He must die

Thomas Scott must die
for raising his voice and his fist
against your provisional government

for insulting your leadership
for hindering the peace with Canada
for boasting once too often

he would destroy the halfbreeds
lead them like buffalo
over the edge of a coulee

see to it the thundering earth
would break
every last one's bones.

You give no last moment reprieve
as you blow your warm breath
into your cupped, shaking hands

and watch his blood spread
a stream over the snow
an image to torture your dreams for years.

5. THE VOLUNTEER

Fifteen years ago Jack Henderson
spat at your shadow when he says it fell
across the jailhouse door:

Louis Riel, I'll be
the one to put
the hangman's knot under your ear.

He claims you locked him up
in Fort Garry. He swore vengeance
for his compatriot Scott's execution.

True to his word
he has slept with hate his lover
these fifteen years to tell you:

Louis Riel, do you
know me? You cannot
escape from me today.

In how many daydreams has he rehearsed
pulling the lever, releasing
the trap where you, trembling, stand?

For this simple use of his hands
he'll be paid fifty - eighty dollars —
the exact sum is not clear.

He says he doesn't want the money
only the satisfaction
of sending your body straight to hell.

6. CIVIL SERVICE

That cutting accent may belong to
no man here, the voice
an unseen stranger's

shouting in the Ottawa Valley
echoing across the Laurentian Shield
bridging the Red River near St. Boniface

following the CPR tracks as a whistle
steaming across Manitoba into the Territories
stopping at Regina and becoming a whisper

in your hooded ears. The enemy
is always too busy to meet you.
He will not face you now

only send
his message to you
across the surveyed distances:

Louis Riel,
do you know me? You
cannot escape from me today.

His name doesn't matter.
It never has. He hounded
you into exile and out of exile

into insanity and out of insanity
into obeying Dumont's call to return
and act upon the grievances of your people

now the people of Batoche, St. Laurent, Prince Albert
now the people of the North-West
Indians, Métis, Whites

into the realization
no grievances would be heard
by indifferent official Ottawa

into exasperation at petitioning the invisible
into desperately leading as David
your people against Goliath

into defiance into seizure
of stores and rifles
to uphold communal dreams

into civil war with all odds against you
into defeat into jail
a prisoner before the Queen's tribunal

where as God's servant you implored
for the last time to be heard
the peaceful longings of your people

for a new order on the prairie
beneath the dancing lights of heaven
with the singing spirits of God and earth

while other Christian strangers
more conscious of the fashions of the day
tried you at last for the murder of Scott

and called it treason against Her Majesty
called it Insurrection
and sentenced you

to spend your last moments of dignity
under a white hood — on their
dark gallows.

7. THE BEAST

And this voice may not be human
at all. Haven't you
heard it before, heard it scratching

in the shadows, waiting to murder you
for serving your vision, heard it
in the wind growing hands like bare branches

promising to strangle you
after shrouding you hearing
in one last grotesque whisper:

Louis Riel, don't you know
me? You
cannot escape from me today.

8. THE LORD'S PRAYER

Remembering your farewell
in Montana one year before
to Father Eberschweiler

and now Father Andre
weeping nearby, believing you a saint,
while you repeat your true Father's words:

Our Father who art in Heaven
Father do you see that tree
on the hill there

Thy kingdom come
Father I see a gallows there
Thy will be done

and I will hang from it
for I have seen
the hour of my own death

I have seen
a flock of dark geese hovering
and shadows on the snow.

9. THE UNDYING

At least half the world
waits for fulfillment
an end to endless dying

while your body plummets
into the dark valley
your spirit rises, no part of it broken:

I leave neither silver nor gold
am on the threshold of eternity
do not want to turn back.

10. THE HORIZON

What appears to be
a lake sizzling below the sun
will dry up when we reach it.

The fields will crack under our feet.
We say this is a myth
so we do not have to believe in it.

Our science separates us, cuts off
our brain from our dreaming heart,
makes us worship at the altar of fact,

finds our children guilty of feeling,
sentences our poets to death
for visions. By denying our blood

is mixed, too, of pain and rapture,
water and earth,
we see our love also silenced

into fear and hate,
all of us condemned to live
under the white hood, the harsh sky.

E.A. LACEY
Saudade

It's cold this morning in the country of the sun.
A south wind is blowing in from Argentina.
The sky is overcast: the pastel-coloured high-rise apartments
look pallid, suddenly dirty; the sea at Copacabana
is as ruffled and gray as Lake Superior.
Only one tired prostitute still patrols Atlantic Avenue and she might
    well be a beggar.
The bars along the avenue have shut their doors and lowered their
    awnings against the spray and the wind.
The ice-cream men with their tinkling carts and bells,
the lemonade and mate salesmen bearing silver drums of drink,
the brown young surfers with bleached hair and salt-smeared faces,
the oblivious lovers gently masturbating each other under coloured
    parasols
are all hidden away somewhere, leading their other lives.
Garbagemen in gray uniforms are raking up yesterday's ice-cream
    sticks and safes and semen,
an old gray man who by the looks of him must be an Anglo-Brazilian
    is being walked by a large excited police-dog along the sand,
and I hear the snow-country calling.
Calling to me in a wind which isn't even coming from the proper
    direction
"reviens, come back, reviens".
Calling as it's been calling, faintly but patiently, for 10 years now,
always in my ears, never quite letting me go
"remember, souviens-toi. Je me souviens...".
Remember my empty spaces, my gray winds and skies, my fields
    of endless snow in an endless winter,
my silent people, whiter than snow, colder than winter, stiller than
    the whispering pines.
my telephone lines humming in the ice-wind, vibrating across great
    prairies, across a continent, from one storm-whipped sea to
    another, carrying messages to nowhere,
remember my solitudes, my countryside
where you can walk for a whole day without encountering a single
    human being,
remember my beaches of rock, my lakes, blue and cold as the sky
    they reflect, deeper than sleep, larger than countries.
remember my forests, dark and inscrutable as night, denser than

jungles, where a man can be lost and never found again.
Remember white death falling from the air in geometric lace,
remember Wendigo, the walker of the snow,
remember the white owl sweeping from the north on wings of
    storm,
remember loup-garou, the howl of wolves on indigo nights, the
    carcajou that kills for lust.
Remember moonlight blue on ivory snow, sharp leafless elm-tree
    fans, red of rose-hips on an ice-fingered bush, snowberries white
    against whiteness,
remember winter flocks of cedar waxwings sudden in the scarlet of
    a mountain ash,
remember etched frost flowers gold in the morning sun on the
    windows of your childhood,
remember how your breath silvered the air as you went out on
    winter mornings, and the reddening slap of cold against your
    face,
remember the walks to school through snowdrifts tall as houses,
    touching the telephone wires,
remember the smells of chili sauce and stew when you came home
    on winter evenings,
remember how, when you came in from the cold, everything would
    glow pink as roses and your fingers tingle, thawing,
remember the green, even in winter, of pine and spruce, cedar and
    fir and tamarack, the green which never abandoned you.
Remember sugaring parties in early spring, the smells, steam, heat
    of the maple-syrup sauna,
remember the sudden congealing of the amber liquid on the crust of
    snow with which you ate it, cold and sweetness intermingled,
remember wild-strawberry-picking in June, kneeling among the
    squashed, elusive, aromatic fruit,
remember wild raspberries in summer, fragrant on the tongue,
    dripping from dusty roadside bushes,
remember the crisp taste of apples gathered in country orchards
    gone wild, on fall afternoons,

remember getting drunk for the first time on heady, homemade
  cider.
Remember the flash of silver blades on blue ice as the red-jacketed
  skaters whirled effortlessly in unending circles,
remember skiers falling bright as autumn leaves down undefiled
  winter mountain-sides,
remember autumn leaves falling down red and gold as tropical
  flowers into winter,
remember and return.
Come back, mon fils, come back,
come back to the bleak barless streets of small Ontario and Alberta
  towns,
come back to my gray Russian cities, hives of isolates,
to my restaurants where a man can't have a drink,
to my bars where a man can't eat a meal,
to my "beverage rooms" where a man can't stand up to drink,
to my taverns where a man can't lift his voice to sing,
to my laws, my laws, my endless rule of law,
my "don't, can't, mustn't, shouldn't, may not".
Come back to the Criminal Code, to the Provincials, to the RCMP,
  to the Morality Squads, to a nation of policemen,
come back to gray youth, bald age and unreadable newspapers
  which are not printed on Sundays,
come back, above all, to Sunday, drinkless asexual church-going
  Sunday, day of the dead in the cities of the dead.
Come back to hockey, to rugby, to the Grey Cup, and to teenagers
  and farmers who would rather curl than copulate,
come back to Queen Victoria's birthday celebrations and the St.
  Jean Baptiste Society's annual parade,
come back to a land whose only rebels fled, when defeated, to the
  United States
and whose only heroes were hanged and exiled failures, or decorate
  boxes of chocolates.
Come back to a schizophrenic national anthem that says two
  contrary things in two different languages, and a flag that is only
  five years old,

come back to Queen Elizabeth II on every stamp and on the
   backside of every coin,
come back to the only country which cannot amend its own
   constitution.
Come back to non-nationalism, non-patriotism and a stake in the
   Yankee slaughter and the Yankee dollar-bill,
come back to the richest of underdeveloped countries, to the land
   that has always refused to be anything but a colony of somebody,
come back to lack of decision, lack of definition, lack of conviction,
   lack of direction, lack of pride, lack, above all, of feeling,
come back to bilingualism, to biculturism, to complete non-
   communication in two languages,
come back to a people who still consider that their true nationality
   is that of the ancestors who came from Europe generations or
   centuries ago.
Come back to the herds of mindless Unitedstatesian tourists sailing
   the lakes of Americo-Canadian Muskoka, tramping the streets of
   Franco-American Montréal, eating hot dogs steames, all dressed,
come back to the carbon-copy tourist camps, motels, drugstores,
   trailer-parks, chicken shacks, used-car lots, and even national
   issues and crises,
come back to Macleans, Saturday Night, the Globe and Mail, the
   Canadian Forum and the Canadian editions of Time and the
   Reader's Digest.
Come back to the edge, to the fringe of things,
to where life has always been pain and pain has been noble,
to the hardness that begins inches under the grass or tundra,
to the cities that huddle for warmth along the American border,
to the abandoned farms of Saskatchewan and the dying fishing
   villages of the Maritimes,
to the wilderness that encircles every town and city like an enemy
   surrounding a camp,
to the highways that peter out above Sudbury and Edmonton,
to the loneliness that anaesthetises the soul,
come back, come back, reviens, je me souviens..."
It's cold today in the country of the sun.

RETURN FROM MONTANA

PLAINS CREE

DAVID GODFREY
Thirty One: Influence

Youngest son. Youngest daughter. The lake in the mountains. Firm joy. When all goes well, courtship remains the image. The dance of the young without arrogance. No false pride among the wise; the good man learns from all who approach him. All.

Six at the beginning. The new idea comes slowly into the world. Feet tingle, that is all.

The influence shows itself among swayers, changelings. Wait until the firm are moved. Injury.

The thighs burn. Holds to those who follow whims, obeys the capricious, ignores all inhibition. Humiliations.

The heart makes no propaganda. Receives none. The CIA eventually jams its own broadcasts. Influence cannot be consciously willed. The strain exhausts; only those closest are affected, at great cost. Remember Lord Sutherland and his enemies. Dumont does firmer work now than in his agitation.

Stiff necks. Influence which affects the firm woman through inner equilibrium has great effect. The will attends to details of the whole.

Tongue wagging. The jaws move rapidly and the good remain un-affected.

DAVID GODFREY
Forty Nine: Revolution

Fire in the lake. Revolution. When your day comes, you are believed
      Remorse disappears; you have honoured the people.
Fire in the lake. Make the seasons clear. The time for Duplessis
      passes. The time for Vallières and Drapeau also.

Wrap yourself in the buffalo's hide. Walk most slowly. It is not
with thunder you move the herd to the people. Can you go slowly
enough? Obey the situation, not your television image of what it
      should be.

Starting brings good fortune. Have you seen clearly what it is you
      bring about? Are the people really ready?

Why did Riel wait so long in Montana? Why did the FLQ begin
before the people were ready. There is a time to strike, a time
when the talk has gone around three times only. Then you will be
      believed.

Nine in the fourth. Men and women believe, knowing what is just.
      The form of no government is permanent, of no class.

The great man moves clearly in the patterns of the people. Their
      wishes are clear as the deer's tail. No need to go to the pollsters.

True, the lesser men will change only their faces. Do not
expect too much. Do not expect Mrs. Bata to rush about serving
the people. Her blood is full of self-deception. But feed the
people well and they will eventually laugh away her fevers,
      sequins, garrottings.

JAMES A. MacNEILL
A Métis Child Dies

Where are the men
The men are dead
And the women
Lie rotting
In clay sheets

Where are the children

White fences
Cradle their graves

Did the rocks weep
Is the wind ever sad

Flint scratched inscription
"Safe In the Arms of Christ"

        christ

This is a book of sorrow
Of blood

Hunger in a bitter paradise

AL PURDY
Canadian Spring

Forests are dark and leafless in March
the morning sun then hesitates then peers
around its own lessening shadows
where brown grass has green memories
But there's some mistake
—by afternoon the day darkens
again and water deliberately
assumes its icy alter-ego
Spring is a series of advances
and retreats but always
edging farther toward the sun
and you think how terrible
it is to be trapped
in a perpetual graveyard
where everyone looks at everybody with pity
or fury if they luckily escape

That dark forest is superimposed
on the Gringo Trail where I'm wandering
in Peru and Pachacuti the Inca conquerer
alternates with Big Bear and Crowfoot
in my mind mangos are puritanically illegal
and grenadines a sexual aberration they
emerge from piles of dirty snow
in Canada but llamas on the *altiplano*
too morally superior for enthusiasm
about anything much less human beings
pause for the camera
whose reverse image is rabbits preparing
for survival by doing and doing
what rabbits do best here
Machu Picchu slumbers another thousand years

Advance and retreat retreat and advance
spring comes sideways spring comes slowly
lilacs imagine their colour is purple
trilliums make up their minds to be white
tolling winter hesitates at street corners
ding-dong spring is silent temporarily
but people are less unpleasant to each other
bars on the prison widen slightly
to re-admit escapees and mayflowers
—my collar is a fuse to prevent strong feelings
my life has a tourniquet holding back freedom—
but rivers slash their wrists
a thousand rivers roar one instant only
sea-wide forests fill the near horizon
forests are banners sprawling green
birds build nests inside this one-time prison
birds are coloured bells
—and it's summer

Cuzco

RAYMOND SOUSTER
The Heroes

Not Wolfe or Montcalm
not Mackenzie, Papineau,

not even Riel
loveliest loser of all!

But Hull of the lightning shot,
old ageless Number Nine
with the shiftiest moves of all,
O bull-charging Rocket,
phantom Pocket,
the Big M with his eagle's glide—

these are our heroes,
born of hockey wars,

we who never quite grew up,
who carry our first sticks with us,
still shooting pucks
from cradle to the grave!

RAYMOND SOUSTER
Found Poem: Louis Riel Addresses the Jury

Your Honours, Gentlemen of the Jury:
it would be easy for me today to play insanity,
because the circumstances are such as to excite any man
and under the natural excitement of what is taking place today
(I cannot speak English very well,
but I am trying to do so
because most of those here speak English),
under the excitement which my trial causes me
would justify me not to appear as usual,
but with my mind out of its ordinary condition.
I hope, with the help of God,
I will maintain calmness and decorum
as suits the Honourable Court, this Honourable Jury....

Your Honours, Gentlemen of the Jury:
if I was a man of today
perhaps it would be presumptuous
to speak in that way,
but the truth is good to say,
and it is said in a proper manner,
and it is not without presumption,
it is not because I have been libelled for fifteen years
that I do not believe myself something.
I know that through the grace of God
I am the founder of Manitoba;

I know that though I have no open road for my influence,
I have big influence concentrated,
as a big amount of vapour
in an engine. I believe
by what I have suffered for fifteen years,
by what I have done for Manitoba
and the people of the North West,
that my words are worth something,
if I give offence I do not speak to insult...

As to religion, what is my belief?
What is my insanity about that?
My insanity, Your Honours, Gentlemen of the Jury,
is that I wish to leave Rome aside
inasmuch as it is the cause of division
between the Catholics and Protestants.
I did not wish to force my views
because, in Batoche, to the half-breeds that followed me,
I used the word *carte blanche*.

If I have any influence in the New World
it is to help in that way,
and even if it takes
two hundred years to become practical,
then after my death that will bring out practical results,
and then my children will shake hands
with the Protestants of the New World
in a friendly manner.
I do not wish these evils
which exist in Europe to be continued
as much as I can influence it, among the half-breeds.
I do not wish that to be repeated in America,
that work is not the work of some days or some years
it is the work of hundreds of years.

My condition is helpless,
so helpless that my good lawyers
and they have done it with conviction
(Mr. Fitzpatrick in his beautiful speech
has proved he believed I was insane),
my condition seems to be so helpless
that they have recourse to try and prove insanity,
to try and save me that way.

If I am insane, of course I don't know it,
it is a property of insanity
to be unable to know it.
But what is the kind of mission that I have?

Practical results.
It is said that I had myself acknowledged
as a prophet by the half-breeds.
The half-breeds have some intelligence.
Capt. Young who has been so polite and gentle
during the time I was under his care,
said that what was done at Batoche
from a military point of view was nice,
that the line of defence was nice,
that showed some intelligence.
It is not to be supposed
that the half-breeds acknowledge me as a prophet
if they had not seen
that I could see something into the future.
If I am blessed without measure
I can see something into the future,
we all see into the future more or less.

As to what kind of prophet would I come?
Would it be a prophet who could all the time
have a stick in his hand and threatening,
a prophet of evil?
If the half-breeds have acknowledged me as a prophet,
if on the other side priests come and say that I am polite,
if there are general officers, good men,
come into this box and prove that I am polite,
prove that I am decent in my manners,
in combining all together you have a decent prophet...

I am glad that the Crown has proved
that I am the leader of the half-breeds
in the North West. I will perhaps be one day acknowledged
as more than a leader of the half-breeds,
and if I am will have an opportunity
of being acknowledged as a leader of good
in this great country....

...If it is any satisfaction to the doctor to know
what kind of insanity I have,
if they are going to call my pretentions insanity,
I say, humbly, through the grace of God
I believe I am the prophet of the New World....
The only things I would like to call your attention to
before you retire to deliberate, are:
1st. That the House of Commons, Senate,
and ministers of the Dominion who make laws for this land
and govern it are no representation whatever
of the people of the North West.

2ndly. That the North West Council
generated by the Federal government
has the great defect of its parent.
3rdly. The number of members
elected for the Council by the people
make it only a sham representative legislature
and no representative Government at all.

British civilization, which rules today the world,
and the British constitution has defined such Government as
this is which rules the North West Territory
as irresponsible Government,
which plainly means that there is no responsibility,
and by the science which has been shown here yesterday
you are compelled to admit it,
there is no responsibility, it is insane.

Good sense combined with scientific theories
lead to the same conclusion.

By the testimony laid before you during my trial,
witnesses on both sides made it certain that petition after
    petition
has been sent to the Federal Government,
and so irresponsible is that Government to the North West,
that in the course of several years besides doing nothing

to satisfy the people of this great land,
it has hardly been able to answer once
or to give a single response.
That fact would indicate lack of responsibility
and therefore insanity complicated with paralysis.

The ministers of an insane and irresponsible Government
and its offspring the North West Council
made up their mind to answer my petitions
by surrounding me slyly and by attempting
to jump upon me suddenly and upon my people
in the Saskatchewan. Happily, when they appeared
and showed their teeth to devour, I was ready;
that is what is called my crime of high treason
and for which they hold me today.
Oh, my good Jurors, in the name of Jesus Christ
the only one who can save and help me,
they have tried to tear me to pieces.

If you take the plea of the defence,
that I am not responsible for my acts,
acquit me completely, since I have been quarrelling
with an insane and irresponsible Government.
If you pronounce in favour of the Crown,
which contends that I am responsible,
acquit me all the same.
You are perfectly justified in declaring
that having my reason and sound mind
I have acted reasonably and in self-defence,
while the Government, my accuser,
being irresponsible and consequently insane,
cannot but have acted wrong,
and if high treason there is,
it must be on its side
and not on my part,

your Honours, Gentlemen of the Jury.

PATRICK LANE
For Riel in that Gawdam Prison

When Dumont rode with his army
there were only muttered words
of praise at the end; the possible
Messiah praying in his prison...

    and how he danced in the circus
    waiting for the clowns to dismount
    while hucksters sold his legend
    to the nickel and dime seats.

There on the prairie there were people
waiting to stop moving. Somewhere
west was too far
and the day eased away into language...

    Indians stumbling over buffalo
    in the ring of Madison Square Gardens,
    Gabriel Dumont riding to the dead
    God somewhere over Regina.

bpNICHOL
The Long Weekend of Louis Riel

FRIDAY

louis riel liked back bacon & eggs easy over   nothing's as
easy as it seems tho   when the waitress cracked the eggs
open louis came to his guns blazing   like dissolution
like the fingers of his hand coming apart as he squeezed the
trigger
            this made breakfast the most difficult meal of the
day   lunch was simpler   two poached eggs & toast
with a mug of coffee   he never ate supper never ate after
four in the afternoon spent his time planning freedom the
triumph of the métis over the whiteman

SATURDAY

louis felt depressed   when he got up he sat down & wrote a
letter to the english   there was no use waiting for a reply

      it came   hey gabriel look at this shouted louis a letter
from those crazy english   they both laughed & went off to
have breakfast
            that morning there was no bacon to fry
      its those damn englishers said gabriel those damn white-
men theyre sitting up in all night diners staging a food blockade
      louis was watching the waitress's hands as she flipped the
pancakes spun the pizza dough kneaded the rising bread & didn't
hear him   its as canadian as genocide thot gabriel

SUNDAY

the white boys were hanging around the local bar feeling guilty
looking for someone to put it on   man its the blacks said
billie its what weve done to the blacks   hell said george
what about the japanese   but johnny said naw its what
weve done to the indians
                                        outside in the rain louis was dying
      its always these damn white boys writing my story these
same stupid fuckers that put me down try to make a myth out of
me   they sit at counters scribbling their plays on napkins
their poems on their sleeves & never see me
                                                         hell said george
its the perfect image the perfect metaphor   he's a symbol
said johnny   but he's dead thot billie but didn't say it out
loud   theyre crazy these white boys said louis riel

MONDAY

they killed louis riel & by monday they were feeling guilty
maybe we shouldn't have done it said the mounties as they sat
down to breakfast   louis rolled over in his grave & sighed
      its not enough they take your life away with a gun they
have to take it away with their pens   in the distance he could
hear the writers scratching louder & louder   i'm getting sick
of being dished up again & again like so many slabs of back
bacon he said   i don't think we should've done it said the
mounties again reaching for the toast & marmalade   louis
clawed his way thru the rotting wood of his coffin & struggled up
thru the damp clay onto the ground   they can write down
all they want now he said they'll never find me   the mounties were eating with their mouths open & couldn't hear him
louis dusted the dirt off his rotting flesh & began walking
when he came to gabriel's grave he tapped on the tombstone &
said come on gabriel its time we were leaving & the two of them
walked off into the sunset like a kodachrome postcard from the
hudson bay

118

CRAIG POWELL
Sunday Morning in St. Boniface

That first winter
here   learning to survive
in Canada   we flex
our high school patois
at Mass in the French quarter   abruptly
shaken and skinned
of our history   after
I question the locals   "Où est
le tombeau de Louis Riel?"   no-one
answers
                    Yet he is here
with a low fence keeping the snow
from his stone   the bells
come loping at mid-day   the hanged
leader   the hanged leader of someone
else's rebellion   I almost understand
that I am happy   nearby
the ice groans quietly where the
rivers meet and I have lost
my hunger to be young   cars
creak on the winter road and a fresh
wreath on his grave foretells
defeat almost a century gone
can be believed in   this
gladness perplexes me
as though I had spoken
something in a poem as random
as our being here   together
or separate under the ruined
cry of this cathedral
plotting rebellion   planet
of savage crystal   listening for the
last battle that will consume us

ANDREW SUKNASKI
Gabriel Dumont and an Indian Scout Changing Coats
for mick burrs

old antoine ferguson
born 1884 in st laurent saskatchewan
antoine remembering the old story
his father told before him
"there was this fog everywhere one morning
and gabriel dumont
he always use to get up early and go for hunt
but this time he went looking for horses
and all at once he heard this howling
something like a wolf
in those days there were wolves
but gabriel he realized this was no wolf howling
it was an indian
the indians they had this habit in those days
they signalled to each other
and they could understand
what they were saying..."

old antoine explains how dumont quietly ambled around
until in a clearing in the mist
he glimpsed the indian scout on a hill
dumont then slyly making a half circle
to ascend the hill
finally sneaking up behind the kneeling indian
the scout with cupped hands amplifying his message
while a knife lay at his feet
dumont seizing the knife
flinging it far into the mist
then swiftly grabbing the indian
one arm round his neck
old antoine explaining precisely
"...the indian really got scared
because he was positive gabriel would kill him
that was what *he* would have done..."

however gabriel assured the indian
"no...it is not our style or mine to kill
unless we have to
we don't kill for nothing...
but when you get back
you tell the others
'i met this man who had every chance to kill me
but let me go...' ''
the indian replying
"nobody will believe me"

gabriel finally suggesting
"to prove it really happened
let's change coats...you take my coat
and say 'this man did that!' ''
"no!" winced the startled indian
"they might shoot me
you know...another coat coming in!"
dumont laughed "no...they won't
not if you're alone"

and they changed coats
dumont murmuring
"by this jacket then
they will believe
it's *really* true
i could have killed you
but didn't..."

dumont
his own dreamer
and mythmaker

ANDREW SUKNASKI
Blood Red the Sun

blood red
the sun sinks to its knees on the edge
of the smoky plain
the pale moon grows older again
and the cree are told
they must learn to walk the white man's road
big bear's spirit is troubled
since returning from the northern hunt
he takes long lonely evening walks
and thinks of the great wheel of buffalo
no longer turning through the seasons
the sun grows heavy
and older
days become cooler while families grow hungrier
their clothes more worn
and ragged
the glow of women's faces
gone
like the light once mirrored by stones
no longer burnished
by the buffalo
shedding old fur
stars fade in the children's eyes
wandering spirit is speaking
"we come here to fort pitt
come for meat
we come for this thing *money*
we wish talk about these things
kapwatamut*..."

*kapwatamut: cree nickname for thomas trueman quinn, trader at hbc post in
fort pitt (1884).

122

ERIN MOURÉ
Riel: In the Season of His Birth

  1

  Riel: *'I hear the voice*
     of the wilderness coming
     out of the north to meet me.'

prisoner
ponders nicked edge of
photo grass behind is not
yet knee-high
wavers toward beard blurred
mouth eroded by spring poplars
budding sunlit each limb warped
& silent w/ old war
river a flat white
banner against his shoulder neck
& cheek dissolve in shadow
grey as autumn Riel
    It is already May —
    You are in the wrong
    season
    Oh where are your armies now

fingers extend thru creased
pockets palms stiff &
flat against thighs
his wrists revealed

white as broken ice tho spring
will not come to Riel
prisoner of autumn when seasons
became film turned silent
behind his neck
hair fleckt w/ dead

leaves frozen
words lacking sound
as he waits now for white -
lettered FIN to blot final stills   awaits
blank screens   projected flips &
clicks

prairie grass too   halts
in the silent milk of his stare

    2

    Riel: *'I see a gallows*
          on top of that hill, & I
          am swinging from it.'

Riel   the voice flickers
just past your mouth   thick
w/ membrane & unable to
reach you   images lengthen/
distort your opened eyes   Riel
      The grass twists at your
      neck
      Oh where are your armies now

the white horseman fades
fleckt on the painted
screen   alone
against ice-crusted river
& reining toward solitary plains
the troops behind you in confusion
turned to poplars upon hill

    Oh where are your armies now

Look behind you   Riel
across water where seasons trespass
urgent   a child born
in autumn ages gains beard
finds slow cheeks crumpling
to prairie

They are hanging a man
but you are not there
either—
instead stand sloped alone
watch black hangman black
priest in wild craft thru
thick glaze of light

the dead man's head hooked
in chalk-white cap   clad black
coat over shirt   wool nettling
flesh   The embracing is long
over now   wrists
pinioned against spine
moccasins scraping gibbet
The window unbarred
prayers finally ended

Oh where are your armies now

3

from the dark river
of your brain   the man Scott
stumbles up   canvas-shroud in patches
torn against his cheek   eyes
unbandaged head no longer
bleeding   bullet-wounds white & dry

stains gone from march snow
leaving only the prints of his knees
& fallen shoulder

blood gone also from spring snows
of batoche
of duck lake   leaving only accusations —
words of the priests
spoken against you & the air too thick
w/ sour gods
for reply

    4

priests & deputies blurred
overexposed   surround gallows
on the poplar hill
surround the man who turns
but cannot warn you   his mustache dark
mouth & eyes eaten too quickly
by shadow
      Why do you watch   Riel
      He is already dead   voices
      knotted in cellulose
      movement/sound
      arrested

      Touch him   Riel
      Reach thru viscous prairie but
      you can't tear this final
      caul   your white fingers leave
      no mark

5

They hang a man & you
are not there   you join
        w/ autumn rivers   ice congealed
        grey at the edge
        your face/beard webbed
        w/ droplets

as trap door jerks down
w/o dangled crack
snapt neck   the man still
leaning fixed in light

        Oh where are your armies now

        Riel   waver thru the death-
        gelled dawn   november returns
        to enfold you now   noosed &
        windless   rivers slowing
        w/o energy
        poplars frozen on hillside
        brittle behind your eyes

while before you   there is this
commotion   your brown-locks clipped
crucifix knocked into dirt   crowds
mumbling in an aftermath
outside the gate   words
you cannot speak nor find
        suspend in thick morning haze
        You gesture madly twitching
        yet the armies fail
        to recognize you   Riel

6

Months later   you
regain spring   as march ice
heaves & back-ends   thawing
finally to movement
        & you drop   delivered
hollow in soundless light down
down thru wooden
trap   face still snagged w/
cold leaves
        You plunge deep
        into hillside which does not break
        your falling

        dark body arcs down &
        down   release from the prison
        of autumn birth   & still
        you are falling   Riel

but your voice dangles
wild & liquid   focussed
as grass reborn
        to breathe in the white spring
        of prairie rivers

DON POLSON
Canadian Heyday

The little
I know of
those gentler times
I discovered
recently

in yellowed clippings
from an attic's
dusty bible

that give a full
but droll account
of the picnic

and that crazy
Frenchman's
public hanging.

GLEN SORESTAD
The Ravens

After the dust had finally settled
after Middleton's victorious militia
had quitted their zareba near Batoche,
taking with them what they had brought,
all they had plundered, and Riel besides.

two black-garbed sisters from Batoche
flapped about the empty encampment,
alert eyes probing the trenches,
darting through the trampled grasses
as they scavenged for left-overs,

seizing a cast-iron pot, an old tea kettle,
a cheap tin fork, discarded or forgotten,
a battered cup whose owner no longer needed
the early morning chill dispelled with tea,
removed forever from military routine
by a shot from Gabriel Dumont's rifle.

GLEN SORESTAD
Archaeologists at Batoche

Summer sun burns a hole
in their patience and they sweat
fiercely, slap mosquitoes, here by the river
these bare-chested shovellers
of history's bones.
They have dug and measured
measured and dug for a month now.

I could have told them.
I could have warned them they'd find nothing.
Their coming has been anticipated.

Long before they arrived
everything of value was gathered, moved
everything of value — every pot, every letter
each bone fragment, each voice, each dream...
Nothing remains but grass whispers and sun.
Even coyote has not passed this way in some time.

Everything is safely stored downriver.
in the cave screened by saskatoon bushes.
You think because coyote sits nearby grinning
it is just the den for his mate's pups?
Do not be so easily deceived.

GLEN SORESTAD
Fish Creek

On a grassy riverbank clearing near Fish Creek
where Fred Middleton was humbled by Dumont
some Métis sharpshooters and a few Indians
a small gravesite, staked square with metal palings
and anchored by a solitary monument
remembers in guarded bureaucratese
the death of several of Middleton's militia.
There is no mention here of other deaths
no suggestion of defeat of a superior force
by a raggle-taggle band of illiterates.

But almost a hundred years later this site
still embarrasses, rankles like an old wound.
It is a secluded reminder of the attempt to forget
a notion supported by the lack of road signs
and the little-used dirt trail to this fact.
These imply a conscious desire to forget
a people, to write their history like Pravda.

A few miles downriver towards Batoche
the spire of the Métis church leans against sky
an indisputable backdrop of truth to history's lies.
In the softness of summer night at Fish Creek
fiddle sound floats on the night wind
ghosts dance on the banks of the South Saskatchewan
sashes leap like flames of blood in firelight
and yes, people do remember, there are too many ghosts
and their graveyard much too large to hide.

E.D. BLODGETT
for ducks
provincial museum, edmonton

1

certain ends cannot be known, but to be
cortés, to seize aztecs in a glass net,
to say, 'now it will snow,' and watch the snow
start and fall and stop — who would not want
to sit with cortés, after all the blood was washed
up, staring at the snow falling over mexico

all white? as if every road i ever walked
took me here, to see the prairie grass as it might
have been, all roads ending in museums where light
like the snow of hernán cortés falls across at will
the thin sloughs and painted floors of grass
where antelope may have run, memories of ducks,

and snakes wrapped in their dreams of rabbits,
burrows cut away and pressed against the glass.
i wanted to weep, and what tears that fell
formed translucent pearls on my cheeks. perhaps
cortés returned to spain encased in glass
drops, and no one saw, for he shone like a god come back.

2

such long afternoons you would say i'd become
walt whitman under glass, loafing and loving, gazing
at the gentle bodies of men and women and children
who gaze at me as one staring into void,
strolling through nathan phillips square before
they are all gone into dark, all
forgotten, brooding through the endless summer
afternoons. 'whose generation is mine?' i wanted
to ask, 'and what should i recall?' somewhere

i wanted to walk where the wind leaves the grass
unmoved, and perhaps then i shall see my friend
of so many other decades ago.

    (o, let me be sly
    when he goes by:
    i shall rise and bow
    the way they showed us how
    when he and i were boys,
    and we would make no noise,
    and none should see
    but he and me)

but where do they go when the light is gone?
is it i alone here, here where the small
windows are closing over canada, waiting
for them all to return, passing hand in hand?
perhaps i should sit with eagles, the glass marbles
beneath their brows chilling in the dark. here

valleys are quick to reach: a step down
and you touch the wall of other mountains, other
streams where under the shaded lights of day
they fall losing themselves. say, will they see
me here, beside the sweet and silver stream,
gazing at silence and the perfect world?

3

better to say: 'walt whitman it is
not, nor ever could have been.' these
windows are time foreclosed, and after them
all appears as negative — the washed air, the shades
of other antelopes surfaced across a slough,
slow mirages exposing.

how many ducks among the reeds, cold and bloodless,
heads gone forever, and only their split tails
placed broken on the floor of water, how many ducks,
and what mouth wailing *quaaa*, stopped in midstream,
its time removed? such ducks as i had seen moving
through small waters near batoche, batoche

where holes spattered on the rector's wall open
to the white sun as light passing through film
falls against a screen. how have i entered this
bloodless space, where are the rifles and faces
shot away, retreats and other rites? what time
do these other ducks move through, echoing

up the saskatchewan, all noise theirs?
how near they come to move as angels move,
simulacra of ducks to say what ducks would be
if there were ducks to see. o, as they pass,
ask them: 'where are the roads that lead to batoche,
what roads to canada, where are the forts, the glass

wall around the plains of abraham, and what has not
cried *quaaa* turning to glass?' batoche beyond
the ends of roads has gone, so platonic
now in the endless beginning, not to be seen
but as shades cast in the endless light
of saskatchewan, beyond ducks and into panes of air.

4

nothing now to do but lie down with ducks,
ducks without name, ducks in the little sloughs,
and ask: 'do ducks get lost?' and hear them feed
serenely in the grass — to know whether birds
playing and feeding in the gentle reeds, should ever
see themselves as ducks flattened on the water's face.

DAVID DAY
Captain Kilroy Was Here

Four miles from camp

on his back
on the white wind-ribbed earth
clenching
    a black pistol

eyes

open
mouth full of snow

DAVID McFADDEN
The Opening of the West

Two crows and a hawk are fighting fifty feet
above the Ontario-Manitoba border
above the line where the great shield
breaks and the trees disappear.
The hills crumble into rocks
and the rocks stop and start again
and isolated stands of poplar
become fewer and smaller and shorter
like the last little islands at the
end of the earth
                   and the low winter sun
radiates everything with prairie fluorescence.

I thumbed a ride into Sioux Lookout
in a tractor trailer on a rainy midnight.
I had to help the guy deliver lumber
at various camps around the Lake of the Woods
then fell asleep in the cab
and when I awoke I looked at the driver
and he was asleep slumped over the wheel
at 60 mph. "Hey wake up!" I yelled and he jumped
then said "Just resting my eyes."

Then another rig pulled up alongside
on the two-lane Trans-Canada
and they began racing, the only
things on the road at dawn, this
flat geometric heaven
or some other supernatural zone
treeless, where you can see forever

and then when you get there
you can still see forever
or as Al Purdy says you can look
forever in any direction except down
and for amusement the angels
pick up hitchhikers and race each other
across the bottom of the sky
and I got a little lonely and scared
and wondered what they were doing
back in Ontario

and I thought if I had to live here long
I'd become a mirror image of myself
and slip through a crack and vanish
which seemed a scary proposition at the time
being a rather unmetaphysical kid

and in recent years I've flown across this line
many times, noting it's not marked
on the world's largest map, that map
they unroll beneath you as you fly
and the prairies look no flatter
than the 3,650 mountains
of British Columbia

and I heard an old Inuit in Tuktoyaktuk
say he'd visited Ottawa once long ago
and it was just like a dream he sighed
a heavenly mist in his one good eye

and now yes it's just like a dream
everything that is even meeting by chance
that well-known saviour and holy man
Jesus Christ during a train stop

in Capreol which is 572 miles north
of Toronto and 635 east of Winnipeg
Winnipeg where a mysterious old African
is spending a long afternoon sipping
slow beers in a downtown pub
the same African who forty years ago
shot down Capreol Red, the most bastardly
CNR bull of the Depression,
Capreol a tiny decimal point
on which so much depends.

And now with Jesus disembarked
in Winnipeg, I promised to write
and wondered where we'd meet next time,
the sun is setting west of Brandon
setting right in my face
and my upper torso is all aglow
not to mention my lower,
I wished I'd taken notes on the
endless stream of stories Christ told

Protesting he's not a teetotaller
I mean a good storyteller
we all know he's not a teetotaller
although he tries to go easy these days
because of an ulcer condition, and nights,
and he's not supposed to eat
anything with seeds—
God, Christ told some great stories
and great imitations of Pierre Trudeau
and of an Indian woman
who sounded just like Victoria Reindeer
of Fort Smith
                    Jesus became
the spirit of the prairies to me
and I told him about meeting a guy

who said he liked to take his horse
and spend weeks loping around the
        Cypress Hills
shooting rattlesnakes and eating them
after roasting them over hot prairie coals
in the evening with the western sky
changing colours

and Jesus said rattlesnake? Why rattlesnake?
There's a lot of prairie chicken in them
        Cypress Hills

and he said how in Sioux the word *manitou*
means both God and Prairie
and how even the Indians were somewhat
alienated from the land
and had to use animals as intercessors
much as Christians use himself.

And I saw young Jesus growing into
some kind of narrative sage (if he lived)
long done with the foolishness
        of holiness
and we looked similar, talked
almost the same although born
almost a world apart
and each of us in his way
tampers with the boundaries
between history and life

yet the epic wanderings of Paul Kane
and the everrotting corpse of Louis Riel
lie in him, not me,
and the great buffalo herds spring
back to life in him, not me

and he kept talking about how he
almost didn't take this train from Ottawa
where he was guest speaker at a convention
of descendants of the Chinese coolies
who built the great Canadian railroad
and how various coincidences developed
that made it impossible to take the one
he wanted, his grey eyes holding mine

and we embraced and I confessed
that at the funeral of a dear friend
a few days before, a death
that for two nights had kept me awake
more than the train's rocking and whistling
I had regretted never having embraced him
and never having told him
how much I loved him
in a completely asexual way of course
because I was afraid he'd think it
queer
          and Jesus, though slightly
embarrassed, returned the embrace
and talked of how he embraced his father
after a long absence

and he spoke of how all this public speaking
was developing into a chore

and how he's getting sick of catching
small fish in the Rockies around Banff
and how he wanted to come to Northern Ontario
specifically the million lakes north of Sioux Lookout
and try to catch a twenty-pound rainbow trout

and just then the West opened up

and a tight flock of birds so high
they looked like a cluster of decimal points
suddenly scattered.

MIRIAM WADDINGTON
The Visitants

At night you think
of your friends the dead;
they sing to you
in a choir of stone voices
and you want to tell them
old stories more ancient
than you mortally know,
all that you fleetingly
surmise shimmering
through the hole
in the foliage of the
nearest tree.

Oh those voices of stone!
Those earth-stained voices
those murmurings in wood
those singings in grasses
those soundings and turnings
on the pathless prairie:
my father groaning and
Gabriel Dumont staring
blindly into the camera
of his own fate.

Those anguished visitants:
they come to dissolve
the emptiness,
they come to console
your cries they come
with their firefly lanterns
to lead you amazed
through their blazing
gateways of stone.

GEORGE BOWERING
Uncle Louis

1

They told us all of Canadian history
took place along a river back east

& now they gave us a prime minister
with the name of that river.

It was my first experience
with the Laurentian Shield. I felt

really debarred. It had been bad enough
to have a prime minister

whose last name was the same
as the monarch's first name.

At least to my south they sported
a true man & told us he ruled

the roost where eagles were bound
to return. Uncle Louis was a poor

relative to Uncle Sam. Back east, I knew,
they loved him because he was so dull.

One assumes that the rhymed couplets are meant to give the inauspicious subject a certain
cachet, a semblance of the consequential the poem so sadly lacks.

Meanwhile, the (spurious) message: small-town western boy is treated as neglected colonial
by Central Canada — really, isn't that growing a little thin? Next he will be carping about
freight rates.

2

Prime Minister Louis St.-Laurent & his new cabinet
are all solid-looking men with thin lips

pulled straight across the lower parts of their faces,
sensible pointed black oxfords planted

on the figured rug on the floor of Rideau Hall,
striped trousers & vests, perfect for nineteen forties

black & white photo. Behind them are two doors
with circular windows, where waiters in white

will soon emerge, carrying roast beef. It will be
overcookt, & Canada will be finishing

the world's most romantic year completely unknown,
again unknown, the tulips taken in again,

we will be just what the Dutch trust. Uncle
Louie, I kept saying, is that you? I lookt

for him the most unusual of places, under
a manhole cover, in a tall Siberian Elm

The unacknowledged source is presumably a photograph of the Canadian cabinet, which
we have all seen in a history text. We know that people the author's age grew up in a
Canada that was supposed to be chronically dull. Is that any reason to perpetrate the idea
with a dull poem?

Al Purdy, at least, would have had Mr. Pickersgill peeing in the rose bush after the
investiture banquet.

3

Louis St.-Laurent was an eighth-generation
Canadian, & so was his brother Nil. In Lawrence, British

Columbia, we knew nothing about Canadian generations,
our fathers & grandfathers from either Britain or

the Balkans, that defined the differences. We were not
British & they were not Columbians, our mothers

served peas & carrots, theirs ladled up cabbage.
Louis St.-Laurent was a complete surprise,

the Prime Minister had always been Mackenzie King,
a sort of bantam Winston Churchill, a fifth figure

in the wartime conference photos. Louis' first-generation
ancestor was Nicolas Huot, whose father's first name

was Laurens. He was a sheriff, not a saint,
& pretty soon his name was Huot-St.-Laurent.

I often went those days to the river to weep,
but not to draw, & not a name, not Bowering-Okanagan.

It really looks now as if the poet is reaching into any source bag to keep his poem going. Every post-1967 poet and playwright in the country has been rifling the pockets of all our dead historical figures. Too bad Louis Riel didn't live in Lawrence, B.C.

And why doesn't he work in the Churchill River? It rises in Saskatchewan & dies in Manitoba, just like Riel.

4

1948. Humphrey Bogart shot at me & barely missed.
Lou Boudreau hit a line drive over my head.

St.-Laurent met with Lester Pearson in Caucus.
The New Look was rumoured to feature ankles.

Bonapart's Retreat gave me a hard-on in Math.
Louis & Jeanne celebrated their fortieth anniversary.

I wrote a history of the NHL with paste & scissors.
Jan Masaryk leapt to the cobblestones in silence.

Duplessis stole the Polish art treasures for Quebec.
Franz Kline painted in the hues of statesmen's shoes.

It was the greatest year in the history of man,
& if you were born right you were twelve.

A factitious assemblage of events if I ever saw one. This fellow could profit by taking some lessons from James Reaney, both in the area of nostalgic history and realization of childhood mythos.

I somehow do not feel deprived of wonderful memories just because I was not born in 1936.

One cannot help being of the opinion that there is no great *frisson* achieved here just because the author once played ball with a French-Canadian boy who shared the PM's rather common first name.

5

"St.-Laurent himself was full of doubts and questions
in the days following the convention." E.J. Pratt

was alive but he wasnt writing any more,
no help there. The CBC was busy with Shirley Harmer.

Louis went to the river to pray. "You gave me a name,
give me a clue!" he demanded. The river flew by

filled with American sludge. It was an answer
but Louis had already turned his back.

He carried his load to the cross on the "mountain."
There he bent one knee & said, "I got inspiration

& spiritual being from you, now how about a sign?"
After he'd begun his descent a dozen bulbs burnt out

& the rest formed a rude lily flower. Three nuns
on the island noted the bloom, considered it the work

of the Archfiend, & swore one another to secrecy.
Uncle Louis went back to the Rideau, offered himself

to Paul Martin, whose eyes lookt this way & that.
"Do we also single out leaders because they will

dishonour us, because they will diminish us?"
We need more doubts & fewer questions, no saint.

The author runs a very great risk in quoting from a poem so much more momentous than
his own. Dennis Lee should sue for unlawful confinement.

One recoils at the necessity of pointing out that Father Brebouef, as seen by Pratt, is
neither a miracle worker nor a fool, but rather a beautiful loser. Perhaps the writer of
this poem should have chosen George Chuvalo as his central character.

6

They called him DDE, after HST & FDR,
but how could you do that with Uncle Louis?

You couldnt ever ask him to take you to the fair.
He *was* the fair. He was in the shadow

of Alexander the Great. Perhaps this is how history
goes, by way of names not enunciated.

You did not say Fred Rose, he fell under the shadow
of the initial fright in the hearts of a certain

Quebec darkness. It was not fair, what they did
to Fred Rose, & so you see, history is not fair,

is *is* a fair. At a fair you throw rings at
bottles & you never ring a bottle. You are training

to be a Canadian, a nice blue suit & you too
can be in St.-Laurent's cabinet. Lockt in, the key

thrown with bottles into the river. Bottles filled
with the river filled with American sludge. There

is the ABC of living in Ottawa, under the shadow
of a B-29. The numbers rise, ever less lucky,

but the letters stay the same. & Fred Rose
in prison, they dont allow him any letters.

If he wants to write a sestina, why doesn't he write a sestina?

If numbers and Letters are really so important, why doesn't he make more of punctuation?

What is a hyphen, anyway, punctuation or spelling?

7

"It would take more than that to banish me: this is my
kingdom still." Under the stone laminate

of that city & all our cities Uncle Louis shoulders
his responsibilities; down the flushes of our rivers

his euphonious syntax flows, 1948, 1949, 1976,
the great trombone of his mind issues forth, growing

Food for Thought between the toes of all who dare to
walk the furrows of his soil. Margaret Sand Laurence

reclines, a backdrop mountain range behind every
town on the prairie, where 1948 was 1907.

She is the cantakerous niece of Uncle Louis, daughter
of the earth he enriches. Salal takes hold on her slopes

& Uncle Louis is working on his first tree. In Canada
we move a little slower, half of us wear mustaches,

one in three has now seen a moose, we move slower
but we build a peaceable kingdom from which

no one is banisht if he can continue to appear Dutch.
Ludvig Van Laurentz gave this earth to us, poems

grow from it like tulips along the riverbank,
they find another dumb name from our history &

spring it as a title: Riel, Mackenzie, Champlain, King.

So at last Riel does make it into the poem, in a comment about the exploitation of national
insecurity, which strikes the reader as tiresomely ironic.

The linking of those names, Laurent, Lawrence, Laurence, seems contrived, one must
say. It is as if the poet believes that subjects in the living world are not as interesting
as the mere words that are employed to name them, or indeed, as if the words and names
are sufficient subjects in themselves.

8

Imagine a country in black & white, imagine
a coast guard cutter sliding down the slips

in black & white, easily assuming its space on the river,
imagine Uncle Louis & Ike on a golf course in peace time,

discussing their scores, each filled with private shame
about "patriots of Hungary and other lands under

the cruel Russian yoke.'' Imagine if you will an angel
named Archibald Lampman puzzled by a pipeline

running between his feet & then south, gorged with ancient
blood, oh my, says Mr Lampman's ghost,

the Soul that from a monstrous past, from
age to age, from hour to hour, feels upward to

some height at last, & filled with terror, falls
into Pennsylvania, there to be encanned & dumpt

into an old man's golf cart, while parachutes bloom
over Suez & Mr Eisenhower says harrumph,

I count you six on this hole, Frenchy. Imagine,
in black & white, the antennae grope for Buffalo TV,

as holes appear in Buda's walls. It is not
Uncle Louis' fault, the world is undergoing drama,

the PM is making memories we'll all forget.

Again, what irony that Mr. Lampman's iambics offer a sweet stream of soul's provender,
flanked as it is by the hobbled anapests of Bowering's maunderings about political life.

As usual, it is difficult to imagine what Bowering's political ideas are, if indeed he has
any. Is he pro-American, pro-western, or just anti-everything?

9

In Greg Curnoe's serigraph the entire cabinet
sits around a council table, each presenting the face

of Mackenzie King. I see Louis St.-Laurent speaking to
the assembled house, a yawn appearing above every chair.

''Grow old along with me. The best is yet to be,''
he is saying. ''But Jesus H. Christ,'' says a petulant

socialist back-bencher, ''the last time you were here
you said the twentieth century would belong to Canada.''

(You should have told him, Louie, this is the twentieth
century, nor are we out of it. How do you like it now,

gentlemen?) The PM drones on, his voice I remember
now, it is grey gravel spilling over agate, covering it.

It is the new plastic garland he carried off the plane
home from Hawaii. It is the one-dollar haircut

he heard about from Premier Frost. Deanna Durbin
turned every word into a dimpled smile on film.

Parliament deliberated. The St.-Laurent cabinet sought
machinery for negotiation. Pearson stifled a yawn

& lookt forward to his new magazine with action shots
of the Cleveland Indians. Imaginary parachutes

blossomed over the St. Lawrence Seaway, bap, bap.

With his penchant for dropping names, perhaps Mr. Bowering should have aspired to gossip-column assembly rather than verse. One wonders whether he believes that the Proper names will give his writing a surface glamour. It is a marvel that he did not direct that the names be printed in bold face. One wonders how much it would set one back to have one's name included in his next effort — or how much more it would cost for the more attractive option, to ensure that it be omitted.

Parachutes, imaginary or not, do not go "bap, bap." They may go "thwuff, thwuff."

10

It used to bother me to hear Saint in a person's name,
even in the juicy rhythm of Louis Saint-Laurent.

(I mean who could respect a Lawrence Saint-Louie?
Or beat him on the back with "Uncle Larry".)

Remember, a kid grows up with names that will later
rhapsodize his childhood. The Whistler knows the secrets

hidden in the hearts of men & women, my daughter
will remember that her young Canada lay

under the uncoordinated footfalls of Joe Clark. I say
"Louis St.-Laurent," it sounds like the authority

of a premier creator of cologne water. My Canada
looks from a cruising wide-body jet like the visage

of Louis St.-Laurent. It looks like prose in a tweed
three-piece suit, the plane lands at Malton, & the

wheels bounce, & they sound like dull rubber saying
"Bounce bounce Bow bounce bounce."

                                    So, my daughters, you

see me going to the cabinet & taking out hundreds
of little bristly white mustaches, pinning them on

the faces of my life, pinning one on George Chuvalo,
one on Foster Hewitt, one on Paul Anka, one on
Barbara Ann Scott.

I wonder whether I am the only reader who is irritated by the fact that this poem seems
to be going nowhere in particular. It could as easily have been set out in one hundred
numbered sections, or four. A poem without structure is like a body without a skeleton;
no amount of mock-sophisticate propping will make it stand up and look capable of
intelligence.

You see? George Chuvalo finally showed up, too. He is the true centre of this poem, though
he deserves better, because unlike it, he was able to stay on his feet against the best of them.

11

Then, I held her in my arms, & told her of
particular status for Quebec, of Quebec &

her many charms. I kissed her while the fiddles
sounded the national interest, Duplessis smiled &

played the Bonaparte's Retreat. All the stars were
generally unfavourable to the settlement, Quebec was

bright, as I held her on that night; & heard her
first minister say provincial priority, & Uncle Louis

say, please dont ever go away. I was dancing
in the Windsor Hotel on October 5. St.-Laurent emerged

with my sweetheart, to the Tennessee Waltz, when
they booed Labour Minister Gregg [who was just]

an old friend I happened to see. I introduced him
to the Parliamentary Press Gallery to announce the news

to my darling, & while they were dancing, my friend
minimized the importance of that aspect of the
disagreement, &

stole my sweetheart from me. Hold me close & hold
a serious discussion of the factors underlying their
dispute. Hold

me fast. A magic spell you cast. It is
between the two conflicting viewpoints, Fred Rose.

The suspicion will not go away that this section was compiled by John Robert Colombo.
It is certainly the most interesting part of the whole literary effort; but it is not poetry.
It may be song lyric and it may be political biography. It may be fun (at least for the compiler),
but it is not poetry. One remembers that our author's recent "poetry" book was stuffed
with quizzes, lists, baby babblings, and random quotations from better writers' fiction.
He should be reminded that he publicly promised several years ago that he was no longer
going to attempt verse.

12

I am done on this side, turn me over,
he said, & sang in the heat. Here, I'll move over

& make room for your new saint, he said,
a wonderful man to give another half his bed.

Here we have the ultimate demonstration that when a contemporary versifier uses end-
rhyme he sacrifices persuasive argument. In this instance our poet employs perfect-rhyme,
and suffers no attack of compositional inspiration at all. It would take an indulgent parent
to tolerate this unsustained overweening assumption of a metaphorical bond between
Rome's St. Lawrence and our own.

One can only be thankful that future generations of Canadians will never have heard of
this piece, because it is too long for the highschool anthologies, and too wretched to be
reprinted in any other forum.

ELIZABETH BREWSTER
At Batoche

Batoche...
a strange wild name
(a trader's nickname, really
but sounding like a battle-cry)
a fierce trumpet name
like Hastings or Culloden.
Battleground once, now peaceful
at the sound of summer wind in wild grasses.
A long drive to it, through green country
and Sunday-dozing towns.
No great battle anyway, I suppose:
a handful of soldiers,
a handful of halfbreeds
fighting over a godforsaken country.
Anything settled by it? Maybe yes, maybe no.

A busload of tourists
views the battle site.
They walk two by two
under the trees
or down a flight of stone steps
to Gunner Phillips' grave.
I know nothing about him,
don't know why I imagine him
just turned nineteen, rather tubby,
devoted to his mother, shy with girls,
a non-drinking Ontario Orangeman.
(Could be forty and a bigamist.)
Patriotic? Needing the pay? He lived too early
to save the world for Democracy.
but maybe thought
he was saving the West for the settlers,
or avenging Thomas Scott.

At Batoche itself
the church is closed for repairs
to make it just the way it was
at the time of the battle.
In the rectory-turned-museum,
where the marks of the bullets are still visible
under an upstairs window,
there are relics of the past
filled with that strange pathos
of unimportant objects
that have survived their owners:
cartridges, guns, hammers,
a soldier's tin plate
battered out of shape,
somebody's diary,
portraits of Riel
and Gabriel Dumont.

Folk heroes maybe?
or a parcel of rebels
as my grandfather thought them
and half crazy at that?
(If any relative of mine
fought in this battle,
he was certainly on Gunner Phillips' side.)

In the old graveyard
in view of the church
the children of the victors
have appeased bloodguilt
by erecting monuments to the vanquished.
Wild roses and saskatoon berries
overhang the graves,
and dragonflies cling
to the rose petals.
Pungent scent of sage inhabits the air.

They have come to possess the earth,
Gabriel Dumont and Gunner Phillips,
their friends and supporters.
Their blood, their bodies
(victors, vanquished)
gone underground, turning
to sagebrush, roses, wheat,
clustered purplish berries
and the thin wings of dragonflies.

When
inaudibly
the trumpet of the Lord shall sound
up yonder
above the church and above the wooden crosses in the
    graveyard
and above poor Gunner Phillips in his solitary victor's grave
will it matter who was right (if anyone?)

KIM DALES
Duck Lake Massacre

It was Mitchell
the store-keeper's
fault
he stowed the guns
we just went to retrieve 'em

so Crozier, mounted
on his blood bay mare
roared 'Who's for it, boys?'
and of course we all were
partly because we'd get paid
partly because
we thought they'd be gone

so we rode off up the Trail
to a cavalry two-step
blowing kisses from the sleighs
singing songs about half-breeds

until we were stopped
by the enemy

then Crozier puffed into his mustache
and said 'Good Indians
had nothing to fear'
and ordered them to surrender
the way they had in '73
and '79
and '84
it was part of a tradition

and then one of the damned
guns fell off its carriage
and the other bloody gun
wouldn't fire

and there we are: ninety
men against ten thousand
in the middle of a field
in the snow
and we'd fired the first shot

the rest is history.

BRUCE HUNTER
He Encounters Hostility in the West

        he struts an awkward modern
David Thompson, pen and astrolabe
probe through constellations of human stars

        he is a latter day Louis Riel
writing on the prison's wall:
        Abandoned
        Abandoned by God
to the fate of other men
but he is not taken
by their claims of immortality

        he counts hairs on their pouted chins
sends his chains heated in fury
to curl around their tongues
their ignorance their poverty

        he is the historical man
no hero, merely unconscious
of the dearness of the struggle
aware only of the coming of longer winters
and days not nearly long enough

ANDREW SUKNASKI
Letter to Big Bear

World's Best Coffee
Broadway / W 158th Street
Uptown Manhattan
NYC
April 24, 1979

Big Bear
c/o *NeWest Review*
10123 - 112 Street
Edmonton, Alberta
Canada

Dear Big Bear,

Here at THE MUSEUM OF THE AMERICAN INDIAN
your medicine bundle lies in some dusty drawer. And I must
confess, I came here wanting to look into your sacred bundle;
however, having arrived here now in Washington Heights on
the edge of the Hudson River, it now seems more important
not to do that. After all, Big Bear, some things are sacred.
Your people kept talismans and sometimes certain remains of
ancestors in such bundles. And they say before a long journey,
or for many other reasons, you would carefully open your
medicine bundle. And pray for strength.

I donno, Big Bear, it seems wiser to understand clearly what
lured me here. It seems best to let these things be — part of
those private things on earth. For the truth is, there were
always only two places where the medicine bundle ever went:
one being where the possessor, and all of us, must someday
finally go; the other, remaining in the caring hands of one's
lineage. This place is neither of those. Making it sad.

Best to you,
Mahzahkahzah

CHRISTOPHER WISEMAN
At Fort Qu'Appelle
for Joan

Fort Qu'Appelle, Saskatchewan.
Foreign to me.
Place of Indians and Oblate Priests.
Standing in the Church of St. John,
built in 1885,
built the year men marched north
from here to fight a war.
A dry May. Drought. Dust.
I find a metal plaque in the church wall.

In loving memory
Pilot Officer Peter Donald Graham Stuart
RCAF attached 19 Squadron RAF

Born Fort Qu'Appelle, January 29, 1918
Missing over the North Sea, August 29, 1941

Here, of all places,
the centre of another history, another war,
my early life is thrown straight at me.
August 1941 he died in the North Sea,
August 1941 I lived by the North Sea,
played and swam in its grey cold,
watched the warplanes, counted them
going out and coming back, identified them.
Now this plaque taunts me,
shocks me with what I was.
I remember my father
in his Pilot Officer's uniform.

Then later in the hilltop cemetery,
sweet with lilacs and May blossoms,
by the infant graves, a grave from Batoche,
I find a cross and stop again.

Reg Bates from Macclesfield, England.
Died of typhoid 1910.

And I lived near Macclesfield, too.
Knew it well. I hear his English accent,
flat, northern, echoing mine.

Wars, disease. Memorials, graveyards.

High on this dusty hill,
from deep in a stone wall,
half the world from Cheshire and the North Sea,
I am reached for by the past.
I am welcomed by the dead.

MILTON ACORN
Dig Up My Heart

Dig up my heart from under Wounded Knee
Where it's been living as a root in the ground
Whispering the beat, to fool mine-detectors.
Though there may not be much Indian in me
That fraction was here first. It's senior.
Take this heart to grow a man around.

I shall be Heartman — all heartmuscle!
Strong and of longest endurance
I've acted, thought and dreamt to nurse my will
Proud for the day of the People's Judgement
When vision rides again and all that's meant
Is said and flashed from eyes once thought blind.
Fewer and fewer of us, rest now in silence.

E.D. BLODGETT
Métis

Speak the great names: Fort Qu'Appelle,
St Isidore de Bellevue, Grand Coteau,
Batoche, Fort Walsh, Frog Lake and Cut Knife Hill,
Seven Oaks and the rest of Rupert's Land,
and say what lies there between: bones
the wind gives back, bones of buffalo, bones
of the hunters, bones of Blackfoot, Cree and Blood,
the prairie piled white with hunts, all
bone brothers under sun. Name
me, Gabriel, king of this bare kingdom

of bones, riding and riding through white remains.
Name me, Gabriel, hero of the Wild
West of Buffalo Bill, hero of the great
Staten Island shoot out, me and Le
Petit, killers of little blue balls,
riding and riding through pictures of sage brush and sky,
fighting with clocks beneath the electric sun,
never as we used to fight, waiting,
talking, never arriving though miles and miles
of coulee and plain. And now where the prairie was

Sitting Bull and I and faces in the dark
square off, Chief of the great Hunkpapa Lakota,
dazed in the painted flats, and I calling,
calling: God, will they find us, lost in faces,
before we stop forever, smiling in a glass
cage, where rivers stop, and birds hang
on the sky never moving? My smile is glass.
Everything lies inside me: buffalo run
to ground, streets I never saw where the elms
line faces singing white, singing

"The Stars and Stripes Forever," waiting for wars
and other shows at the town's end. They see
me, Gabriel, and see a war that hardly
was, a circus war so put off we almost
missed the last call. Dummies I gave
them to save my friends, men stuffed like the great
chief and I who drift slowly through places
and then through names where hundreds walk to gaze
and conjure us. Speak the names—me, Gabriel,
a clock ticking to an abandoned house.

E.D. BLODGETT
omphalos

no roads lead from it.
epilogue, palinode, and afterword
all stop

breathless before it.
this is where doing is
unable, the known

unlearnt, this hiatus, this
ecstasy blowing through a wall
where the hanged man sways, beating time.

i want to speak of forgetting,
to speak of in and out, to say
it is one.

i want to tell you
i cannot give my name.
i think i lie beside an old river,

my bones beside other bones.
perhaps my skull belongs to someone else.
no one knows what the year

means, why the centre
is called batoche. it is only wall,
aperture, and timeless, expiratory dance.

KIM DALES
How My Great Uncle Missed Most of the Riel Rebellion

so he says to me
he says
well you know
and I says
sure
so here we are
in the middle of
goddamn who-knows-where
hauling lord-knows-what
for Christ's sake

So when I finally sees Middleton
I asks for my pay
just goes right up
and asks
and he says
Houie
Mr. *Houie, if you please*
I say
well he just looks
me up and down
and he says
Mr. Houie
he says
You're fired.

KIM DALES
Fort Saskatchewan, 1884

My dearest —
We have a new problem:
the Indian agent speaks English and Cree;
the Indians speak Blackfoot and French.
Our MP refuses to comment.

Yesterday
our petitions to appropriate ministers
were answered by a shipment of dictionaries.
Tomorrow the Indians
begin to learn Cree.

DON FREED
Duck Lake

There's a little town a short ways north of here
a speck upon the prairie
And every hand is calloused there
For idle hours are few

    I'd go there as a boy in the long vacation times
    Tractors purring in the distance — horse flies buzzing
    I'd roam my uncle's fields and the sandy roads
    With a sling-shot, my little brother and my cousins

(Chorus)

    In that little town
    With its myth of a rebel
    A mem'ry of a struggle long ago put down
    But it's still around

There'd be people loafing outside the hotel
Seldom speaking — never smiling
Hellish faces holding empty eyes
Like they belonged just to the shadows

    I was reared to fear them — "Donnie don't go near them
    ....they belong on the reservation."
    Even the jukebox in Parrot's Cafe said
    "Son, don't go near the Indians."

(Chorus)

One Saturday night in Parrot's movie house
The whole town was there watchin' Elvis Presley
He slammed a bully up against the juke box
—sang a song on his own terms

    And the movie ended — triumphantly
    There was a burst of applause — felt good to hear it
    And the shadows left with a spring in their steps
    Eyes flashing wide with some special spirit

(Chorus)

POUNDMAKER AND SPLIT MOON

FRANK DAVEY
Riel

1. NICE THINGS

The nice thing about Louis
was that Davy Crockett went south
to the Alamo. The nice thing about Louis
was my mother always called him 'real.'
The nice thing about Louis
was that us smart kids
got to take a classy subject like French
in Grade 9. The nice thing about Louis
was that he'd never appeared on Disneyland,
& looking at him in 1955
from the lower Fraser Valley there were so many
nice things about Louis Riel.

The 'real' rebellion she called it.
I believed her. It hadn't happened in Mexico.
You couldn't play
cowboys & Riels, you couldn't play
Riels & Indians. There was no way
you could imagine it & therefore
it had to be a real rebellion.

2. WACOUSTA

I knew he was not Wacousta.
I'd never heard of Wacousta, my mother
hadn't heard of Wacousta, only,
of the real Louis but we both knew
he was not Wacousta.
Now I have heard of Wacousta I can say
that if Louis had been Wacousta
all the Rudy Wiebe Cree on their piebald ponies
would've come whooping from their tipis. Louis
would've glared up from U.S. postage stamps
wearing feathers & warpaint. Dumont
would've won the second battle of San Jacinto leaving

Middleton's army steaming
in its charred CPR pullmans.
Of course if Jesse James had been Louis Riel,
he'd have been a Red River cart robber,
a survey crew bandit, a pemmican kid.
There'd have been no General Middleton only
a Pinkerton man.

3. TRYING TO THINK OF LOUIS REAL

A raw-boned Canuck in long underwear.
A solemn mouth under black whiskers.
A man from Winnipeg.
A man from Winnipeg which was the head office
of Eaton's catalogue, where my flannel
shirts & corduroy breeches came from,
in brown paper packages, each November.
He did look a bit like Timothy Eaton.
He was dressed in black like Timothy Eaton.
Came out of the black past like Timothy Eaton.
Had not moved history, had been moved into it,
had joined with words like tax man, back east,
Liberals, baby cheque, Royal Bank, Toronto Conservatory,
rationing, Mackenzie King.
He was dressed in black like Mackenzie King.
He had done something and now it doesn't matter.
He had done something but now it wasn't something.
At 4 pm, after I had died several times as an Indian
my mother called me in to practice the piano
& above each piece of music in my practice book
was a small picture of a black-bearded unsmiling man.
There was something wrong with these pictures.
Sometimes the music smiled, or flashed
an orange mustache. The Real Rebellion.
There was something fishy, my mother would say,
about Louis Real.

4. LOUIS AT FORT GARRY

We are not in rebellion against the British supremacy...
Moreover we are true to our native land.

LOUIS RIEL
NOVEMBER 16, 1869

'Oh shit,' Sir John A. said, 'Riel
has shot that Thomas Scott.' Damn Tom Scott.
He was a troublemaker. He shouldn've been born
on a mountaintop. Should've gone south
& run for Congress. Got himself drunk.
Even in Fort Garry prison got himself drunk.
Had once tried to throw the boss of his road crew
into the Red.
Maybe he was an anarchist individualist.
He called Riel a 'dumb frog,' the Métis
'a pack of cowards.'
Maybe he was a fascist running-dog.
He told Louis in colorful Protestant language
to go love the Blessed Virgin.
Louis Riel said, 'He is a very bad man,'
& sent him for trial to a Métis tribunal.
The court found Tom
not up to community standards.
Man, this is one tough city, said Tom Scott.
You can't even have a little drink, a little fun,
even curse out a Frenchie
without they bring on the Gestapo.
There'll be no more American licentiousness.
We must stamp out the Wacousta factor,
said Louis Riel.

5. LOUIS IN HOSPITAL

All month Louis has nightmares. In the nightmare
he prays. 'O God, make me thy prophet,
make your David thy prophet,' he prays.
'O.K.,' says God, & jumps thru the barred window
dressed as a Baltimore oriole.
'What shall I say, O golden & adored?'
prays Louis. 'Say
the 20th century belongs to Canada.' Louis flinches.
'Say per ardua ad astra, say mens sana
in corpore san.' Louis covers his face.
'Say nemo dat qui non habet,' chirps God.
'You're no oriole,' says Louis.
He backs into a corner of his cell.
'You're a Macdonald,' he shouts.
'A tyrant, an overdressed Bismarck!' he screams.
God grins. 'You sound a lot like Col. Crockett,' he says,
then flies off
into the wild blue yonder.

6. LOUIS IN MONTANA

Maybe he wears a six-gun.
Maybe he shoots buffalo.
He's a 'hard citizen,' says the *Fort Benton
Weekly Record*. Maybe he busts broncos.
'He's one of worthless brutal race
of the lowest species of humanity,'
says the *Fort Benton Weekly Record*.
Maybe he's a grizzled old prospector,
maybe he's a scout for the 5th Cavalry.
He writes to Gen. Miles of the Cavalry
asking for a Métis reservation.
He wants them taught to farm.

He wants schools. He lobbies the U.S. Marshal
to have whiskey-traders jailed
for selling to drunken Métis. On weekends
maybe he races chuckwagons.
Maybe he plays poker in the Bucket of Blood saloon.

In 1883 he is hired as a teacher
by a mission school.
He hangs up his six-gun. He unloads
his buffalo gun. Sells
his decks of marked cards. Gives away
his Bowie knife. He is bored.
His old buddies Dumont, Ouellette,
Isbister come down for a binge.
To play the slot machines. To gawk
at the Silver Dollar Bar. Afterward,
flat broke, hung over,
Louis rides with them back to Canada.

7. LOUIS AT FISH CREEK

A tree-covered cut in the prairie grass.
A 'nasty' place
says Middleton, aiming his cannons into it.
Dumont's men enjoy
the dim light of these bushes, sing & pray
as they fight. Meanwhile,
Louis is waiting,
his arms upraised, is praying
for vision. He opens his mind.
'Be allways sure you are right, then Go,
ahead,' Davy Crocket tells him.
'Yes go ahead,' Dumont insists,
by messenger from the battleground.
There must be authority, says Louis Riel.

An authority that loves us, he says.
'Authority ain't worth
the underside of a coon's tail,' says Crockett.
'They've got Gatling guns,' reports Dumont.
'We've got to attack from the darkness, fire
from the trailside hollows.'
An authority must love its people, says Louis
or else the most they can achieve
is to be martyred by that cruel authority.
'You want us to be martyred?' says Dumont.
'Boy, wuz I ever,' says Davy. 'I got stuck
like a bar atta turkey-shoot.'
You were your own authority, you never asked
for love, says Louis Riel.

8. LOUIS AT BATOCHE

Ya gotta choose, said Charley Mair. If ya ain't one of us
yer one of them.

Imagine halfbreed Louis trying to play
cowboys & indians. Palefaces
& redskins. Yankees & rebels.
Or Cornwallis & Washington. De Haldimar
& Wacousta.
Ya gotta choose, said Dumont,
gotta let us shoot, he said,
& afterward headed south to Montana.
Louis kept crossing the border. Down
to Minnesota up to Toronto, to Montreal
to attend school. Down to Minnesota
up to Assiniboia to meet a survey crew.
Pardoning Charles Boulton. Executing
Tom Scott. Down to Minnesota
up to Ottawa to sign the Parliamentary register.

Down to Montana. Up to Duck Lake, Batoche.
Guns sounded. The bullets
went back & forth.
Ya gotta choose, said the billbore man.

Instead, Louis prayed. Moved from house
to horse to house, praying. Moved
from chapel to chaps to chapel, praying.
Nothing was quite right. The Church of Rome.
The wild-west ambush. The Dominion Lands Act.
Statehood. The bullets went back & forth.
To & fro. He prayed.
He prayed for aboriginal rights,
for low tariffs, for provincial ownership
of natural resources, for a homeland
for the Métis, for amnesty, for funny money,
for a railway to Hudson's Bay,
for long skinny farms, for the Crow Rate.
His friend Lepine accordingly had a vision
of valleys and coulees with low houses
shaded by birch trees. Louis said hey,
that's just what we need, & so told Dumont
to go build more trenches & barricades
of birch logs. Then Louis prayed again.
When he was finished praying the bullets stopped
& three Mounties led him away to meet the General.

CONNIE KALDOR
MARIA'S PLACE/BATOCHE

On the South Saskatchewan River
There's a crossing and a bend that they call Batoche
And on the banks of that river
A battle was won and a people were lost

Well they've chased us once
And they'll chase us again
Do you remember Gabriel
"Oui je me souvien"
We have called on Riel
He will speak to us now
"Will you fight for the land that is yours
Are you men?
For the red coats are coming
Well this time they must take with guns
What once they took with a pen

On the South Saskatchewan River
In small little holes the red coats lay hiding
With only the Queen on their side
And Riel he has God and a vision
But it won't fill their guns
So they know in their hearts
That it won't turn the tide

So you run Gabriel
For your vision lies hanging
From a rope, in a jail, in an English town
Yes you run Gabriel
For your skin is worth saving
There are many like you
Who must run from the crown
Run Gabriel
Though your heart it is sinking
When you think of the lives
Of your friends that it's cost
Run Gabriel
And someday you'll return
To the bend in the river
They call Batoche

On the South Saskatchewan River
The crossing and the bend and the banks remain
The people have long since been scattered
Town is still there but it's not the same
But you can hear Gabriel and Riel even
yet They are whispering "you can win
what once was lost."
You can hear it in the rustle
Of the poplar leaves
At the bend in the river
They call Batoche.

KEN MITCHELL
The Nile

Pharoh's armies set the valley
to shake. Even the pyramids tremble.
There — rising over Baal-Zephon —
a pillar of cloud, a pillar of flame.

Naa, Middleton was just a limey, didn't
know his ass from a hole in the ground.
And that so-called army — buncha
Canadians! Farmers *from Bruce County,*
called theirselves reg'lers. Lucky for them
they had a good quartermaster.

A column of dust plumes above the Nile.
Ten thousand peasants from Hyksos appear
in waves, chariots clattering to Gizeh.
Ramses' footmen blanch and grip their axes.

Well our boys weren't so green, y'know,
learned a few things chasin' buffalo.
Only a handful ever shot a guy before,
but with a few Cree and English breeds
we held 'em off two days at Fish Creek.
You could hear 'em talkin' about retreat!

Admiral Nelson and General Napoleon
bare their teeth at Aboukir,
cannonading the delta. A navy of men
lays seige to an army of boats.

You have a look there on top the hill,
where Dumont's grave looks over the river.
That's where we dug the rifle pits,
Streaking up and down like snakes.
Gabriel designed 'em himself — not much
but it stopped the Limey for three more days.

Below the cataract at Wadi Halfa
a hundred canoes arrive from Winnipeg —
Butler with his Cree and Caughnawaga
paddling the Union Jack to Khartoum.

Only ting worried us was the Northcote,
had a machine gun mounted on the deck,
even carried some armour — hah! —
Gabe's stolen pool table. We dropped
the ferry cable on her, mashed the stack.
She drifted on a sandbar all afire.

Rommel's flame-blackened tanks growl
across the dunes to Alexandria
while the Tommies sicken with despair,
picking sand from their boiled potatoes.

When they finally got the cannons up
all they could aim at was the church,
just makin' noise and scarin' the women.
We would of made pemmican outta them but
all we had by then was handfuls
of gravel to load in our guns.

The felahin and his deaf mule
pause in their harness of ropes
watching silver showers streak
the skies above the Nile.

KEVIN ROBERTS
Riel

Riel whose tongue is the tiny
flame of the sacristy candle

Riel whose tongue on paper
demands the impossible
freedom of land and words

against his shimmer the stolid
Loyalist wall

John A and the need for
CANADA
a mare usque ad mare
railway economics
irrational steel lines
denying the natural flow
North/South   geese/buffalo &

people who follow
seasons of flesh

Riel whose tongue slips
along the edge of legal
documents   cuts the tip
drops of blood

Riel whose tongue is the short
snap of flame from cannon

bodies of Métis scattered smoking
to the black/yellow careless
season of grapeshot

Riel who put his mouth on the muzzle
and cried for liberty straight
down the barrel

Riel whose tongue under the white
hood curled like an Autumn leaf
back and in
on itself.

GEOFFREY URSELL & BARBARA SAPERGIA
South Saskatchewan

South Saskatchewan, mighty river
a thousand miles from the mountains to the sea
let us wander your shining water
flowing together, flowing strong and free

Down from the mountains, from giant icefields
sun melting snow in the warm days of spring
comes a beginning, crystal pure water
on rocky slopes with new freedom it sings

Chorus
South Saskatchewan, mighty river...

From the wide river people once gathered
fish from the water, berries from the shore
watching the willows from green to golden
ice still and frozen, then breaking free once more

Chorus
South Saskatchewan, mighty river...

Over the water, Gabriel Dumont
lies in a grave in the fields of Batoche
his spirit flows onward, flows like the river
past into future, nothing will be lost

South Saskatchewan, mighty river
a thousand miles from the mountains to the sea
let us all wander your shining water
flowing together, flowing strong and free
flowing together, flowing strong and free

LORNA CROZIER
Drifting Towards Batoche

Drifting down the Saskatchewan
towards Batoche. The canoe
slips from cloud to cloud
mirrored in the river, sluggish
in the second year of drought.

At every bend, a great blue heron
pulls his heartbeat through the sky,
then disappears in his own grey smoke.
So many herons.
Or is it the same one,
lifting at the sight of our canoe.

The river we travel is the one
Gabriel crossed. The same
feeling rises in my breast
each time I see the heron,
hear the word *Batoche*. A sense of loss
and grief. A distant pride,
though these were not my people.

Past the hills, the graveyard,
the abandoned grey shacks,
the river pulls us into our own
sad century. Ahead, rain clouds
build a darkness we drift towards,
the heron repeating itself
over and over in our eyes.

TERRENCE HEATH
Lament of Madeleine Dumont, July, 1885

Not even a campfire
To warm my chilling body

Madeleine pulls the blanket
around her. The shapes of
four figures lie in a circle
on the prairie — mounds of
horse blankets, moonlit
humps, black in the
shadows.

The sweet smell of horse sweat
The night's dampness
Rises from under me.
No campfire for fear   the police will se us
Gabriel is safe
He will be saddened by the news   I carry
his father's death

I carry bad news
like my mother
Moon-that-hides
Bore her last, dead baby on her back
Looking for a place where his spirit would come
Again
The smell of that decay
was sweet
It flowed out from us like honey
They wouldn't let us near the fort
My father left us on the prairie
I held her skirt in my fist   until he returned
If I had given birth   even
to a dead baby

I would have found him a soul
And sewn it under his skin   like a medicine stone
A young Gabriel   but not so bull-
headed   St. Anthony, pray for us

Old Ai-caw-pow
                  Gabriel's father
                               is dead
He died, sitting in his chair   "The Stander"
Sitting looking upstream from the house
                          a rug over his knees
With his last breath he called me   by his wife's name
And told me where
He had cached the pemmican
By the trail to Fort Pelly
                               forty years ago?
                 A dry bundle of meat, stained
                    purple-brown with chokecherries
Moon-that-hides taught me to dry the dark-red buffalo slabs
And pack them tight in the pouch of skin
                    and her own bundle rotted
My belly hangs dry and empty

                                She turns onto her back.
                                In a few minutes — the
                                night sounds are loud —
                                her coughing begins,
                                phlegmy cough. She turns
                                onto her other side and
                                pulls the blanket down
                                behind her. A figure in
                                the circle shifts. She
                                holds the blanket top
                                rolled in her fist.

But they won't catch Gabriel
He is safe   in Spring Creek
He ran
                                She reaches out and breaks
                                off a grass halm that sticks
                                into her cheek. The slight
                                movement briefly rouses
                                another figure in the circle.

Not even a fire
To warm our bodies and cook our food
Tomorrow night I will see him again
He will be changed   I don't know how
                    he will walk differently
                    his speech will have quickened
                    he'll raise his heavy hands from his sides
                                        apologetically
Old Ai-caw-pow   is   dead
I'd have been a better wife for him than for Gabriel
Gabriel doesn't need me
Ever since I first saw him on the trail near the fort
                    astride his horse
                    (he was like one of the huge posts of the
                    palisade
                    his arms the iron hinges swinging
                    the gates open and closed)
I have felt
                    I was nothing
                    I was small and moving past him
Like a season   like smoke
He was fixed
A point past which we all moved
Not that he didn't move too   He was always moving
                    but it was different
When he moved everything moved
In early summer he left on the buffalo hunt
The winter camp disappeared
Our new home in tents was more permanent
Than the winter house he built for waiting
Than the piles of logs drying for next winter's fires
More permanent even than the mission of St. Laurent
I moved past him like coursing snow water
                    It was always that way
We squatted beside a trail to the river
He built his ferry
                    travellers moved past him
                              back and forth
                              across the Saskatchewan

(If he wasn't away visiting or gambling)
I often felt more like one of the travellers
                    than his wife
I suppose he had other women   I don't know
But they passed too
I used to visit his father Ai-caw-pow

                              to rest
                    from my movement
                              to float
                              on the old man's quiet

But that's all changed now
Gabriel has run away
Everyone says it was the wisest course
David has given himself up
They say he will hang
                    Better he hang alone than with Gabriel
Gabriel is no coward
He faced the Canadian bullets at Duck Lake and Fish Creek
I think he wanted to die on the battlefield
                    a carcass   drying on the prairie
David made Batoche a buffalo run
Why should Gabriel wait with him for the rope?
He ran
For the first time   he moves around fixed
                                     points
                    the Canadian government
                    the people coming to fill the squares of land
                    dead buffalo
He is a wanderer in this land   restless
moving about   doing things   that will be undone
I have to go to him
He needs me
I am the only one that understands the moving
                              having no centre of my own

I reached out and gently rolled the old man's eyelids
over his eyes
        still looking
              at the flowing water
              Madeleine folds her
              handkerchief and coughs
              into it, folds it again
              and holds it wet in her
              hand.
I bring bad news
              She pulls the blanket
              around her body
              and shivers.
I bring news of death
              and death
              becoming fixed
In me as I am borne across the prairie at night
In the early morning and late evening
In the shadows of hills
            like black humps on the prairie
I am a hump   a shadow   becoming night
Oh, Gabriel, are you waiting for me?
           Do you need me now?
The cruel stars say no, as they move through the night sky
The days pass with sun's arcing
But the night is fixed and we move continuously
           around its dark-red fire

WINSTON WUTTUNEE
Ride, Gabriel, Ride

Gabriel on his horse
Sucking hard on the wind
A great Métis of the plain
Riding low, shooting hard
A battle to win
With his people's hopes growing dim
So much depending on him
This man, a war tryin' to win

Scared soldiers screamed
At this giant of a Métis
Scared wild-eyed men on his trail
Crackling Gatling guns
Sang songs of death to Dumont on his horse
Gabriel will take you away.

Ride, Dumont, ride
You can't die, you can't hide
To the battle you must go
Write your name in history
Fight treachery of those politicians so bad
Want to kill you and your land
They're writing their name with your blood

Scared soldiers screamed
At this giant of a Métis
Scared wild-eyed men on his trail
Crackling Gatling guns
Sang songs of death to Dumont on his horse
Gabriel will take you away.

And after it's all done
You can't lose, you'll have won
The respect of all the Métis
Here today in your name
Heads lifted high and our voices will sing out your name
As you lead us in battle again.
The battle is still going on.